Young's Town

A Reverie

Young's Town

A Reverie

Jim Villani
Editor

PIG IRON PRESS
Youngstown, Ohio

Young's Town: *A Reverie*

Copyright 1997 © Jim Villani

ISBN 0-917530-50-0

All Rights Reserved

Published in Youngstown, Ohio

Pig Iron Press
26 North Phelps Street
P.O. Box 237
Youngstown, Ohio 44501

To the People of *Youngstown*
Then, Now, & Tomorrow

Laura Kiriazis

Young's Town: *A Reverie*

Editor & Designer

Jim Villani

Associate Editors

Marlene Aron
Tom Copeland
Chris Flak
Bill Koch
Bill Mullane
Clare Puskarczyk
Steve Svecz

Editorial & Production Assistants

Linda Berteau
Lilibeth Cardano
Kathryn Daly
Jimmy Joe Filicki
Erin Gyomber
Laura Kiriazis
Pat McKinney
Diana Shaheen
Jason Swegan
Susan Wojnar

TABLE OF CONTENTS

FOREWORD

Jim Villani, *A Town Happens* 10

OUR LIVING HISTORY

Theresa Maino Hill, *The Quadrille* 38
Agnes Martinko, *Leaving the Farm* 46
Agnes K White, *Life During the Depression* 55
Pat Mckinney, *Ghosts* 77
Jean Dalrymple Deibel, *Bancroft School* 78
Charles Curry, *West Side Memories* 80
Carol Miller, *Fragrance Makes a Neighborlyhood* 82
Madelyn T Sell, *Grandpa's House* 88
Madelyn T Sell, *Just the Two of Us* 102
Theresa Moon, *Just to Breathe* 91
Joyce Farrell, *The Love Affair* 94
Patricia Olson, *East Side* 99
Dorothy Jones Honey, *A Twenty's Holiday Plan* 104
Dorothy Jones Honey, *The Way it Was* 161
Lucy Hite Murphy & Diane T Murphy, *Memories of Idora* 110
Ruth Merolillo, *Life in the Twenties* 112
Paula J McKinney, *The Snowman* 118
Paula J McKinney, *Home Again, April 1963* 164
Patricia W Cummins, *Fannie, My Friend* 121
Diana Shaheen, *Sarah* 126
Lily M Green, *Peach Blossoms & Galvanized Steel* 134
Khepri C. Polite, *Cat Owner* 137
Frances Duffy Taylor, *Three Hiccups and a Bark* 140
Randy Abel, *Tsunami* 146
Sylvia Centofanti Stefani, *Eighty* 156

ARTICLES and ESSAYS

Lucille Loury Stewart, *I Remember St. Ann Church*...................62
Edith T. Hill, *Belmont Branch YWCA*.................................70
Madelyn T. Sell, *Seventy-two and Still Steppin'*...................153
Edward G. Manning, *Mahoning Coal Railroad Co*......................167
J. Richard Rowlands, *Jeanette Blast Furnace*.......................183
Mary Patrice McGuire Foley, *The Puddler Poet*......................190
Frank Polite, *Take Young Out of Youngstown*........................201
Susan Wojnar, *The Green Man*.......................................222

POETRY

Valerie Esker, *On the Youngstown Skyline*...........................15
Valerie Esker, *Mahoning Valley Memory*..............................17
Valerie Esker, *To West Side Jim*....................................76
Anita Gorman, *Mahoning Valley Multiculturalism*.....................16
Anita Gorman, *My Father's Resting Place*...........................227
Kenneth M. Bancroft, *Legend*..18
Harriet Schwebel, *I Remember Youngstown*............................19
Jim Jordan, *A Childhood Youngstown Adventure*.......................22
E.G. Hallaman, *Noon Hour on Federal Plaza*..........................25
E.G. Hallaman, *No Oboe*..208
E.G. Hallaman, *They Came at Dawn*..................................218
George Peffer, *Youngstown, Ohio*....................................28
George Peffer, *Laundromat/Found Poetry*............................205
Jim Villani, *Old School, Youngstown*................................30
Jim Villani, *Moment in Bronze*.....................................179
Helen Shagrin, *Shirley's Symphony of Sound*.........................32
Helen Shagrin, *Life's Tapestry*....................................230
Lulu Ann Bernardich, *Walk With Me Lord*.............................33
Bill Koch, *St. Columba*...34
Bill Koch, *Lunchtime Special*......................................200
Thomas P. Gilmartin, Sr. *Bring Back the Cross*......................37
Thomas P. Gilmartin, Sr. *Losing You*...............................221
Laura A. Byrnes, *Glenwood Ave.*.....................................98
Juanita Hall, *Wildcat*...106
Juanita Hall, *Scrapbook*...162
Mark Reed, *Ghost Wildcats*...108
Dorothy Jones Honey, *W W I/II*.....................................114

Nancy Bizzari, *The City of No Return*..112
Nancy Bizzari, *There She Is*..115
Rosemarie Policy, *She Remembers*..116
Francie Magnuson Kerpsack, *Steelman*.......................................165
Marguerite Wilbarger, *Extinction*..174
Betty Jo Cartier, *Safety's Sake--For Heaven's Sake*..................175
Perry W. Snare, *Ghosts of Glory*..176
Pamela Sioux Featherston, *Valley of Steel*...............................188
Stephanie Hong Owen, *Ohio Song*..189
William Greenway, *Between Pittsburgh and Cleveland*.............198
William Greenway, *Youngstown*..199
Glenn Sheldon, *Reasons for Maps*..204
Roger Jones, *Special People*...206
Diane Drapcho, *Dancing with Dr Zona*..210
Cynthia Booher, *Starvation*...214
Terry Murcko, *Hey Buddy (A Polka)*..216
Irene Santon, *Futured*..228

SONG

Mary Thigpen Gibson, *Sit Down Child*...60
Mary Thigpen Gibson, *Don't Forget About Me Lord*....................61

ART and PHOTOGRAPHY

Gregory Fesko ....Cover
Laura Kiriazis 3
Chris Yambar 13
Yvette D. Parry 14
Pat McKinney 36
Keith Barkett, *Glacier Drive, Mill Creek*....................................120
Keith Barkett, *Silver Bridge*..145
Keith Barkett, *Jeanette Blast Furnace*...........................178, 182
Josephine E. Minor, *Bag Lady*..136
Suzanne Kane, *Ohio Works*..166
Suzanne Kane, *Butler Museum*..209
United Steelworkers of America...172
Isabel Kiriazis, *Steelworkers' Dilemma*....................................186
Isabel Kiriazis, *Calendar Art*...231
Michael Green, *Keen Eye*...226

Acknowledgments

"Tsunami" by Randy Abel in *Heartlands Today*. Huron, Ohio: Bottom Dog Press, 1996.
"Sit Down Child" by Mary Thigpen Gibson. Chicago: Martin & Morris Music, 1969.
"Don't Forget About Me Lord" by Mary Thigpen Gibson. Chicago: Martin & Morris Music, 1969.
"Bring Back the Cross" by Thomas P. Gilmartin in *Catholic Exponent* 31 May 1996. Youngstown Diocese.
"Noon Hour on Federal Plaza" by E.G. Hallaman in *Noon Hour on Federal Plaza*. Youngstown: Pangborn Books, 1983.
"No Oboe" by E.G. Hallaman in *Noon Hour on Federal Plaza*. Youngstown: Pangborn Books, 1983.
"They Came at Dawn" by E.G. Hallaman in *Noon Hour on Federal Plaza*. Youngstown: Pangborn Books, 1983.
"Youngstown, Ohio" by George Peffer in *Personal Effects*. Warren, Ohio: Bacchae Press, 1993.
"Laundromat" by George Peffer in *Orphan Trees*. Youngstown: Pig Iron Press, 1980.
"Take Young Out of Youngstown" by Frank Polite in *Youngstown Vindicator* 24 November 1995.
"I Remember Youngstown" by Harriet Schwebel in *Youngstown Business Journal* 24 March 1985.
Where's Joe, Bumper Sticker, United Steel Workers of America: AFL-CIO, 1975.

The cover illustration, drawn by Gregory Fesko, is adapted from a photograph of Central Square, downtown Youngstown, circa 1930, courtesy of the Mahoning Valley Historical Society.

In Memoriam

Emanuel G. Hallaman

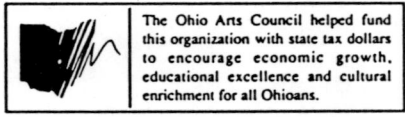

The Ohio Arts Council helped fund this organization with state tax dollars to encourage economic growth, educational excellence and cultural enrichment for all Ohioans.

Jim Villani

A TOWN HAPPENS

Youngstown, Ohio is hardly a natural site for a town to happen, landlocked flood plain nub of earth at the foot of glacial rock creeks, and on a Beaver bound almost river, oh *Mahoning*, oh spittle of Mill Creek, Crab Creek, Dry Run, Yellow Creek, Hines Run, Pine Hollow Creek, Godward Run, Grays Run, oh little lost rolling waterway passing east from Ohio foothills, so useless to the sweep of industry that they had to canal you to make you work for coal, the old pictures showing canal duct and locks and the pulling of barges alongside the old river. In its uselessness, *Mahoning* weeps and pees along its corridor until the iron merchants slab it with chemical wash, let it carry our sins and refuse away. Oh *Mahoning*, to rise pitifully North then fall South not even a map sorts you out; maybe formed vitally in Warren west where Eagle Creek and Duck Creek conjoin, then leaning southward, fed by Mosquito Creek, Mud Creek, Meander Reservoir; or maybe trail your origin west and south to the West Branch wetlands, and industry falls in along an almost river, breathes prosperity, creates a tradition, spawns a people, a people that glow our living history.

What, I ask you, does a wanderer like Young, Indiana bound, a stopover, bequeath us? Frank Polite takes Mister Young to task in the present collection, I yield to Frank, concede his point. This is not **Young's** Town, but it did happen here, a people and a culture did come together here, anchor here, presume a future here. That gives me pause to marvel, pause to reflect on my fortune to be part of a tradition, pause to offer up this book in thank you to all of us, then and now. I need not pen the glamour and prosperity, need not mourn its loss; the essays, stories, and poems I weave together for you do that immensely.

This be not complete as history of Youngstown. We are not all here, cannot all be collected in book form, we are too large, here able just to catch little slips of our lives, some modest reminiscing pleasure, and a rivulet grows into the ocean of personal memory of and gratification for the largeness of it all. Like the neighborhoods our immensity replicates, becomes a mammoth *Mahoning*, a monster valley, and boots along the corridor of our heritage. I walk these neighborhoods, call them up in my poems and my dreams: Federal Plaza, Smoky Hollow, Spring Common, Brier Hill, Monkey's Nest, Westlake Crossing, North Side, Wick Park, Crandall Park, Liberty, East Side, McGuffey, Lansingville, Haselton, Lincoln Park, the Robinson Road Company Houses, Lincoln Knolls, Lowellville, Campbell, Struthers, Poland, South Side, Buckeye Plat, Fosterville, Uptown, Idora, Brownlee Woods, Boardman, Forest Glen, Applewood Acres, West Side, Calvary Run, Bears Den, Kirkmere, Cornersburg, Austintown, Canfield, Ellsworth, Berlin, Milton, McDonald, Girard, Hubbard, even tiny Coalburg, you get the idea, the 'hoods, love 'em all, even those not summoned in reverie.

I applaud my historians for their ability to reminisce on paper, to share that remembering in a permanent way. We look at the past, certainly, at ethnic heritage and immigration; we look at rural upbringing and coming to Youngstown because it is the CITY; we look back to the twenties, look at community in depression -- the economic upheaval the country shared and the psychosis leveled on Y-town particularly with the abandoning of an iron industry; we look at industry's roots, at the Jeanette Blast Furnace, and back as far as the Mahoning Coal Railroad Company, not remembered at all I'm aware; we look at neighborhoods, at schools, at churches, at Idora Park naturally; we look at seniors, at minorities, at parenting, at youth, at vacationing, even at dogs and cats; we look at workers and poets; we look at venerable institutions of memory, like the Belmont branch of the YWCA and St. Ann's Church, we look to the suburbs, at ring communities who sent us theirs; we acknowledge myth, too; remember the *Green Man*, how many of us remember? Remember with us in these pages, look at teaching, at sharing, look at the tapestry of remembering itself.

I am not going to call up my writers and editors by name in this forward, they introduce themselves elegantly in their writing and crafting of this book. Read their baking, and gardening, and tooling in these pages. Remember more than they give, write a piece of your own living history even, if only to share with family and friends, that is enough really. I apologize to those of you who have waited months for me to complete this project. The authoring of these epistles by my writers just begins the process of making a book. For these stories to become *book*, requires many hours of labor, hours of typing, hours of sitting at the computer, hours of editing, page designing, pasting, of printing, collating, and binding. One flips through these pages quickly, not seeing the hours of touching, of shaping. Done now, finally, I offer it to you; relish it, be inspired, and be Youngstown grateful. ■

Youngstown Vindicator
And The Youngstown Telegram

PRICE SEVEN CENTS   YOUNGSTOWN, OHIO, SUNDAY, OCTOBER 18, 1959   **CITY EDITION**

In Today's Vindicator	
Births 2	Porter ....
Bishop 1	Social 18
Bridge 31	Sports 13
Comics ... 31,32	Theaters 7
Deaths 12	TV-Radio ...
Editorial ... 10	Want Ads .. 26
Finance .. 24,25	Weather .....
Parade	

★ ★ ★ ★
The People's Paper
The Weather
today diminishing
tonight
Hourly temperatures from the *Vindicator*

Remembrance of Things Past

SAIGON (AP)—Sporadic fighting, possibly involving fresh Viet Cong troops, flared again today in the Chinese section of Saigon and the enemy hit the capital with a rocket and mortar attack for the fifth straight day.

Doctor Says Kennedy "Was Practically Dead"

ANSWER TO TODAY'S PUZZLE

Crossword

Youngstown, Ohio
Sunday, April 15, 1951

4th Infantry Will Go to West Europe

Washington, April 11—(AP)—The Fourth Infantry Division at Fort Benning, Ga., has been ordered to Europe to become part of Gen. Dwight D. Eisenhower's European defense army.

Safety Record
City Traffic Fatalities
Deaths in last 24 hours 0
Deaths this year 6
This time, 1967 7
Days since last death 55
Fire Alarms in Last 24 Hours
Thursday
12:30 p.m., Juanita and Crandall Avenues, flush street.
3 p.m., 3318 Neilson Ave., woman locked out.
6:18 p.m., near 311 Cohasset Drive, junk auto burning, no loss.
10:05 p.m., Dale Street and N. Garland Avenue, mail box ignited, no loss.
11:36 p.m., 395 Euclid Ave., assist ambulance crew.
Total alarms, 5.
Total damage, none.

Youngstown Vindicator
Friday, June 7, 1968

Book Reviews
Pig Iron Is Really 'Somethin'

McKelvey's

School Levy Is Beaten; Fear Strike

Kent, Ohio (AP) — Protest songs quickly turned to weeping early today as long-delayed construction of a controversial gym began near the Blanket Hill site of the 1970 Kent State University shootings.   Sunday, Aug. 8, 1976

WALT DISNEY'S True Life Adventures

Sheet & Tube to Go On Four-Day Week

Youngstown Sheet & Tube Co. will concentrate the major share of its steel production in the Indiana Harbor Works near Chicago, shutting down a major share of its Youngstown operations. Jennings R. Lambeth, president, announced today.

"This involves" laying off or terminating" approximately 5,000 Youngstown District employees.

Can't Alter Draft Card

The Mahoning County sheriff's office has warned that any person caught using an altered draft card to prove he is 21 will be arrested and turned over to the FBI for prosecution.

Youngstown Vindicator 13
Wednesday, June 5, 1968

the back of the card warns that any person who alters, forges, knowingly destroys or in any manner changes the certificate may be fined $10,000 or imprisoned five years or both," Sheriff Davis declared.

Downtown
PARAMOUNT—"Valley of the Dolls" (color), 1:50, 5:45, 9:40. Patty Duke, Barbara Parkins and Susan Hayward star in the best-seller mixing sleeping pills and show business (A). "Tony Rome" (color), 3:50, 7:50. Frank Sinatra plays a private eye investigating murder in Miami (A)".
STATE—"Cool Hand Luke" (color), 1:340, 9:35. Paul Newman establishes legend by defying a chain gang; "Wait Until Dark" (color), 3. Audrey Hepburn plays a bit attacked by mobsters (M)
PTA LIST—The Motion Picture Council and Parent-Teachers ... classify films as (F), family, (G), suitable for all groups over L. (M), mature young people; (A), adult; (N), no classification received.

Theaters

Drive-in Theaters
SKY-HI—"Wild in the Streets" (color). Shelley Winters, Christopher Jones. 8:11, 11:30 (N); "Nobody's Perfect" (color), Doug McClure, 10:40 (N)".
NORTHSIDE — "The Sand Pebbles" (color), Steve McQueen, Candice Bergen, 8:35 (M); "One Million Years B.C." (color), Raquel Welch, 12 (Y).
SOUTHSIDE—"Around the World in 80 Days" (color), David Niven, all-star cast, 8:55 (F); "Operation Kid Brother" Neil Conner, 11:35 (N).
WESTSIDE—"Here We Go Round the Mulberry Bush" Winters, Barry Evans, 8:55, 1:20 (N); "The Good, the Bad and the Ugly" (color), Clint Eastwood, 10:40 (A).

Camera News

Three Feet of Water Or Don't Bother Us

Usually three feet of water in the basement is sufficient reason to ask for immediate aid from the fire department.

But Friday's heavy rain flooded so many cellars in Boardman that firemen had to set up a priority system, dispatching crews to homes where the water was three feet or higher.

Mental Health Cases Up

Valerie Esker

YOUNGSTOWN SKYLINE

Stark--
against the sky
steel ghost
scrap metal now
once blast furnace
where hot molten iron
smelted into
flaming ingots
seared a place
in history
its cold remains
a disemboweled corpse
odd awkward tribute
to outmoded industry
to hungry men who journeyed
here
to earn a buck
then drink a beer

— Yvette D. Parry

YOUNGSTOWN VINDICATOR

Anita Gorman

MAHONING VALLEY MULTICULTURALISM

Halushki, pierogi, chicken paprikash;
dobos torte, babka, pizelles;
tarantella, tamburitzan, cimbalon, bodhran;
Cultural Diversity.
Decades before the experts recommended
that we don the costume, explore the roots,
name ourselves anew,
we were already dancing and singing,
feasting and laughing,
showing our bright colors to the factory smoke.

Valerie Esker

MAHONING VALLEY MEMORIES

I remember summer breezes
On hot Ohio nights
Blew soft caresses through the window
After Mama dimmed the lights

The heat of each blast furnace
In the valley down below
Where Dad hard made his living
Lit dark sky with orange glow

Death's hand fueled that furnace
With his greed for war machines
But it kept our table loaded
And lulled me off to childhood dreams

Kenneth M. Bancroft

LEGEND

On the spine of Wilson Avenue
closing dusk twists neon,
smoke.
Locals filter through the Paris Inn
to hear fables;
Carbon sparks from black
risen from the valley,
white flux searing air,
for in their youth
it was a vision of brimstone and steel.
As the circle closes,
fathers vow
if you pierce sulfur glare
to the creature's slumber,
spirits toil in amber,
sinew and cinder,
fueled by faith in magic,
children
braced against night on Wilson's spine.

Harriett Schwebel

I REMEMBER YOUNGSTOWN

I've been thinking about **Youngstown**
Quite a lot. But what you see now Is what you've got.

When I was a kid the smoke stacks were smoking;
We'd drive there with my Dad and he'd say to us,
Joking, "When those fires go out,
It means Youngstown is down."
As we sat in the car overlooking the town,
I'd laugh and say, "Daddy, that will never happen here."
And Daddy would say, "let's hope not, my dear."
But little did we dream, my sisters and I,
That it would really happen, I think and I sigh,

Remembering when I danced on the *Paramount* stage,
When intermission entertainment was really the rage.
And my sisters and I would sit in the box
At the *Palace* watching Twentieth Century Fox.
Then Gus Edwards played here
And I danced in his show in the old vaudeville.
I felt like a pro.

The old *State Theatre* near the corner stood,
And *Friedman's* candy store where treats tasted so good.
The old *Hippodrome Theater*--
I danced there, too, in a show called "Chicken Feed,"
For a policeman who had been killed in an accident,
And our community raised funds to help his family,
Youngstown should be praised.
They rallied around and donated their time
In the days when the whole show cost only a dime.

Remember *Clark's Restaurant* and *Petrakase's*, too.
And the old *Palace Grille*
Where Steve prepared for you delicious hot roast
Beef sandwiches, which we devoured with delight
With mashed potatoes and gravy,
How we savored each bite.
And everyone went down to *Raver's* to dine,
To have chocolate mocha cake which was really divine.
To the *V.F.W.* and the *Mural Room*, too--
A trunk of junk for the kids when dinner was through.
Do you remember the *Fish House* for dinners and dates,
And old *Grant's* dime store with twenty-five cent rates?
Shopping at the *Oles Market* or *Livingston's* ladies' store,
I look down Federal Street -- they're not there anymore.

Hartzell's men's store and *McKelvey's*,
The buildings still stand.
And *Lustig's* shoe store, and even the old *Strand*.
Or the *Public Market* where they hollered their wares--
Shouting "Cantaloupes and Watermelons, Apples and Pears!"
Scents from *Hoffman's Delicatessen* and *Ostosh's Deli*,
And the *Italian Restaurant* for pasta and vermicelli.
And let's not forget the *Ohio Hotel* and the *Purple Cow*, too;
After dates -- they were swell.

Kress and *Kresge's* dime stores and the *Youngstown Hotel*,
And the *Blue Ribbon Restaurant* where we'd
Enjoy the smell of luscious roasts on the spit,
In their window we'd gaze; The *Brass Rail*
Was great, too, in those good old days.
Dining at the *Commercial Club*,
To *Jay's* for a hot dog,
Then *Poulako's* for pastry or a hot bun with glaze.
There was *Glickstein's* pet store,
The old *Playhouse* for plays,
And the old *Isaly* stores with 3 scoops for displays,
The old *Central Store* on East Federal Street,
And the *Bus Arcade* where kids gathered to meet--

All these landmarks are gone
And it saddens my heart;
I hope someday **Youngstown** will get a fresh start.
I miss the flames burning from the *Sheet and Tube* mill,
Republic, and *U.S. Steel* -- watching them was a thrill.

Good old *Idora Park* where the Wildcat was king,
And the dance hall would open every spring,
Maybe someday industry will be back--
And the *B. & O.* Railroad will be back on the track,

Let our town see great revitalization--
Let our memories inspire us, inspire the nation.
I've been thinking about **Youngstown** quite a lot.

Jim Jordan

A CHILDHOOD YOUNGSTOWN ADVENTURE

Hard to believe
it was decades ago,
pre airbags and seat belts,
pre malls and cinema plexes,
that two brothers bounced up and down
in the back seat of a two-tone
Ford convertible;
They couldn't sit still
because of a burning sensation. . .
money in their pockets
saved from cutting Grandpa's backyard,
Soon to be spent
on comic books and model cars;
With mom behind the wheel
and Grandma riding shotgun
wearing a pillbox hat with a veil
and dark sunglasses
and one of those mink stoles,
the type with the whole mink nose to tail with beady eyes,
we were on our way to our most serious
shopping expedition,
the frequent trip
from our western PA home
to the area's shopping mecca,
Downtown Youngstown.

To me it was as adventurous
as *Drums Along the Mohawk*,
the music from the Fairlane's one speaker said it was more like
Elvis on Route 7,
further up the road it was
the Beatles on Wick Avenue;
Past dealer after car dealer on the
Wick auto strip,
all the latest makes of Detroit iron were there:
Galaxies, Comets, Starfires, Jetstars, and **Novas**,
Space Age names for the days of JFK's ***New Frontier***;
Each dealership had triangle-shaped multi-colored rows of flags,
to me they conveyed a carnival atmosphere,
little did I know they were there
to scare off birds and their droppings;
Then past Butler Institute of American Art and
picturesque Jones Hall;
Over the hill
and we were in the heart of Youngstown.
On the outskirts of downtown
lay the soul of Youngstown,
the steel mills;
But here in downtown
were stores reaching to the sky,
full of treasures
Marco Polo could not imagine,
Department Stores like *Strouss*
and *McKelveys*
were so big
almost every floor had a restaurant on it.
Strouss had its famous chocolate malts in the basement,
restrooms on every floor,
a plumbing contractor's dream
and a janitor's nightmare;

Elevators and escalators to move you about
seemed like
amusement park rides;
When we parked our car
they lifted it into the air
on a ramp to park it on another floor.
An amusement ride even for the car . . .
an all encompassing experience.
Strouss and *McKelveys* each had a whole floor
with nothing but toys,
pure heaven!
We joined in the hustle and bustle of West Federal street,
past *Woolworths*, *Peoples* drugstore,
Hartzell, Rose and Sons and the **Parkade** Shops;
Mother and Grandma would head to
Lustig Shoes and *Livingston's*;
After taking my brother and me to *Fanny Farmer's* for candy,
they would drop us off at the *State* or the *Warner* Theater,
we would sit spellbound watching movies like
Ben Hur or *The Alamo*,
Then it would be off to the *Ringside*
for some spaghetti
or *Isaly's* for a skyscraper cone;
It was all bigger than life
I can't help but be reminded of it all
when I take my kids to
faceless malls
and crackerbox cinemettes,
I feel sorry for them,
they never had the experience that was
Downtown Youngstown.

E. G. Hallaman

NOON HOUR ON FEDERAL PLAZA

The Home Savings tower chimes twelve times
and swings into a 1940's ballad--
noon hour has begun.

Young lawyers in clusters, three piece
peacocks, talk of torts investments,
and corners to be cut. They scan the Plaza
not with Clarence Darrow eyes--
more like adolescent seducers.

So many women young, not so young,
just miss being beautiful, the stunners
leave for Houston on midnight flights from
Pittsburgh. What's left is not so bad:
nineteen year olds turning fat,
cosmetic junkie runaways from a traveling
mime show sidetracked in Lowellville.

And Sadie, the grand old lady,
volunteer custodian of the Plaza, her amp-
lifted whiskey voice warns little
black kids away from the faded flowers.

Some sit to eat on the coin-shaped
concrete slabs around the broken fountain,
actors in a Coke commercial directed
by a madman. Some carry food to the office,
flat white pizza boxes or torpedo
sandwich bags stained with vinegar oil.

Peanut eaters never sit, their jaws work
as they walk, the rhythmic crap-
shooters motion: shake and throw, shake
and throw.

Men in their fifties, maybe more,
characters from Hopper paintings, pre-
maturely retired, jacked up on Geritol
like predators from Wild Kingdom
wait to put belated moves on thick-ankled
matrons. Conditioned to lose, they
smile at rejection.....and wait.

A monument to steelworkers makes
an ugly bookend. Siegel is long gone
chuckling in some major city, kin to the
con man who sold Garibaldi statues
to a thousand Southern towns.
The rusted openhearth stands cold
tended by a single steelworker, his
partner vandalized by drunken teenagers
hides in Higbees uneager to return.

Courthouse "boys" move amoeba-like
nourished by the lunch special
at The Italian where paper napkins get
chin-tucked and friends gently fight
over the ends of bread.
Wearing out their toothpicks
they return to heel-marked desks
until it's time for handball at the Y.

The hour passes. A breeze that starts
gently high on East Federal, funnels
through a canyon of bank buildings
into a wind that chills
even when the sun is warm.

Stone benches are left
to the old who forget to move.
They watch orange-vested CETA workers
chase scraps of paper across the bricks.

The chimes sound.
Another musical hit, remembrance
when depressions ended
and wars were always won.

Noon will come again.
Tomorrow.

George Peffer

YOUNGSTOWN, OHIO

Home has a finality,
a dolorous ring,
when everything is faded,
banal, obsolete.
The pitted arteries of commerce
carry, here, a sluggish fleet
of bondo-plastered burning wrecks
that travel like clots
towards accidents, and the streets
flush through neighborhoods
that appear abject, non sequiturs--
nothing makes sense.
Old shutters peel, paint weeps,
the broken slats blink, then stare;
whole streets of crooked houses
menace and break on a park
of dark trees, lush as cancer.

The new labor and industry museum is a
mausoleum to dead industry and squats
in an urban pasture
like a gelded bull.
The University and the hospitals
are full, but they send people on
to some place better--
the poisoned river has begun to clear;
it's easier to find the bodies there now.
I think of what Yeats had to say
To a Friend whose Work has come to Nothing:
    "Bred to a harder thing
      Than triumph . . ."
Yeah, bred to nullity and decay,
the black sip we take with every breath--
the unexpurgated, raw, real world
of failure and death
is what we come to face--
is not so easily forgotten here
where home is, daily, a final resting place.

Jim Villani

OLD SCHOOL, YOUNG'S TOWN

Old Dad Tells stories,
Reminisces
Across old world color,
Full barrel Zinfandel
Squeezed Fall-time and coddled
Through winter,
The blood of the neighborhood.

Steeped in new world color,
Bo Peep, from the Hollow,
Steals bicycles
On the North side,
The red steel scud air
Shading the industrial hollow-hood--
You could always buy a bicycle
From Bo Peep for a quarter, full bit.

Now Grandpa, a mason,
His crew of builder colleagues,
And boy helpers who haul brick
In belt-straps early-morning-time,
Carry ladder on trolley,
Ladder stretched along seat windows,
Outside the bus,
Hanging from helper's hands
Trolley front to trolley back,
Full length.

Pop measures son Alphonse,
Breathes across the line of his neck,
His shock of red hair,
The modesty of his flat back
Rigid against the line of seat,
And cautions him,
"First I teach you,
Then I lose you,"

The law of the line for builders
lay on work and family, a garden,
a cigar, a Sunday afternoon of rest,
yes, grandma Alessandrena made no bones
about cigar smoke, banished its tarnish
to the basement where Pop and Zio Mike
sit near the furnace, inhale
the heat of a parodi double-pack,
sip juice glasses of wine,

And years sip away in bubbles,
Fade into liquid stories,
Evaporate into the orality of living history,
Vapored, caressed,
These stories wear color,
Boast, and fill the blue
Corridor of the old school.

Helen Shagrin

SHIRLEY'S SYMPHONY OF SOUND

Once I had a pupil
Whose hearing for her was restored.
She listed the sounds she heard,
Sounds she never heard before.

I took that list and read it
Over and over again.
It seemed to fall into a pattern,
So I recorded it to be reread every now and then.

The flight of birds,
The drone of bees,
The rustle of leaves stirred by the breeze.

The laughter of children,
The crying of pain,
The rumble of thunder accompanying the splashing rain.

The patter of feet
Heard on the stairs.
The voice of self, heard in reverent prayers.

The lapping of waves,
The swishing of grass,
Just myriad of sounds heard now at last.

So from a simple child
A Life Lesson I was taught:
Have empathy and compassion toward others,
For those who bear a heavier lot.

Lulu Ann Bernardich

WALK WITH ME LORD

Give unto the Lord the glory due unto his name;
worship the Lord in the beauty of holiness.
                              Psalms 29:2

Walk with me each day Lord,
As I go about my daily chores,
When I go to my job at the hospital,
Walk with me Lord through the busy doors,
Walk with me Lord into the patient's room,
Some with newborn babies to take home soon,
Others with pain and sorrow,
While their families wait in sorrowful gloom.
Walk with me Lord out on the streets,
Where children and young people go to have fun,
Or their friends to meet, only to be shot down,
By someone on drugs,
Or some other reason when carrying a gun.
Walk with me Lord, as I go out and see homeless
    people hungry and cold,
With nothing to eat and no place to sleep.
Walk with me Lord, as I go to church to worship you,
    and listen to someone preach your Holy Word.
Walk with me Lord as I face each day,
When I try to be good and remember to pray,
And try to help others along the way.
Walk with me Lord until my dying day,
Then walk with me Lord in your home far away.

Bill Koch

ST. COLUMBA

In the heart of Youngstown
between a cathedral and a broken down van
the hulking granite figure
of a saint
waits by the corner

standing barefoot even in winter
a fitting symbol
for the people who wander
into Burger King and stay all day
for free coffee refills

holding a weighty book in his left hand
If he decided to be
a Bible thumper
he could do some serious damage

stretching out his right hand
to bestow a stony blessing on Federal St.
(I'm always tempted to give him
a high five
but don't want to be disrespectful)

keeping a hollow eye on the clock
of the *Home Savings* building
probably unaware
that their t.v. commercials show squirrels
balancing on a tightrope

He dreams for the day when he can
walk down the hill
join hands with Ghost Town Ed
and Mayor Ungaro
and the check-out lady at Rite-Aid
and the poets at Cedar's
and together
they can make **Youngstown**
a place to call home

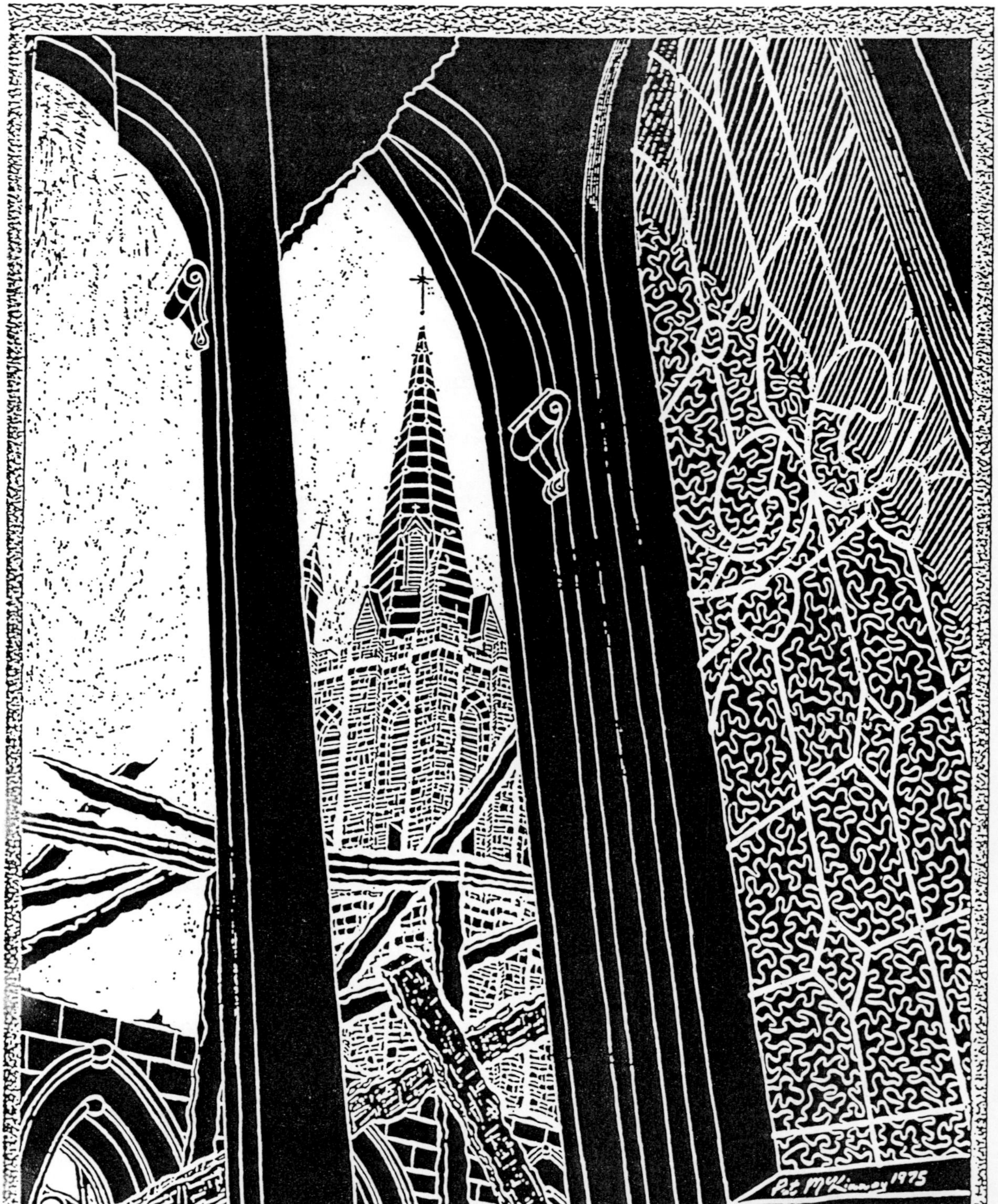
Pat McKinney 1975

Thomas P. Gilmartin, Sr.

BRING BACK THE CROSS

The cross is not a symbol--
Not a metaphor
Not something to look at
It means much, much more;
It is a way of life,
Come follow me
I am the way
My yoke is light
Light compared to sin
Slavery and other worldly things.
Without the cross-- no Church
No Lent-- No Easter-- No Good News
No Victory . . .
Who took the cross
Out of the Cathedral,
It's time to bring it back.

The original life-size crucifix, which had been removed when the St. Columba Cathedral sanctuary was remodeled to accommodate the Vatican II liturgical changes, has been located, refurbished, and reinstalled at the Cathedral. Bishop Thomas J. Tobin officiated at the rededication, Friday, May 24, 1996.

— Pat McKinney

Theresa Maino Hill

THE QUADRILLE
Carmine Maino and Teresa Veneziano

My grandfather, Carmine Maino, was born February 25, 1866, in the rocky hills of Bella, Basilicata, Italy. He was the son of poor farmers, Vito Maino and Brigida Caldano. In 1891, Carmine and his brother Donato came to the United States, first to New York City, then to Youngstown in order to work in the mills. They rented a little house on Meade Street, under the present Division Street Bridge.

My grandmother, Teresa Veneziano, was born on December 8, 1880, the eldest child of Antonio Veneziano and Maria De Luca. The Venezianos came to the United States about 1895 and lived at 391 Division Street. Carmine called on the Venezianos and asked permission to marry Teresa, who was only 15 years old. Antonio and Maria agreed, and on October 9, 1896, they were married.

Although Carmine was notoriously tight, he rented a horse drawn surrey for the occasion. Carmine was never to own a carriage or car in all his life. Teresa wore a long gown of maroon faille with leg-o-mutton sleeves, a matching picture hat, and a parasol. They were married at St. Anthony de Padua Church.

Carmine and Teresa set up housekeeping in the little house on Meade Street. They started their family with Bridget, born in 1897, Mary, born in 1898, Antoinette I in 1900, Rose in 1902, William in 1903, Antoinette in 1905, Nicholas in 1906, Christine in 1908 and my father, Joseph, in 1909.

Carmine was short and husky, and had brown hair and eyes. His hair turned prematurely gray when a young man. Teresa had brown hair and blue eyes, but their nine children had brown eyes like Carmine.

The little house on Meade Street had only two rooms, a kitchen and bedroom, with an outhouse in back. When Carmine's mother, Brigida, visited, she would sleep with their two little girls, Bridget and Mary. The grandmother Brigida was well under 5 feet tall and she and the girls would sleep sideways on the bed. There were two beds in the room with a blanket separating the marital bed from the children's. Teresa had her fourth daughter, Rosie, in 1902, but the baby died nine days after birth because, it was said, she knew her mother didn't want another girl.

In September of 1903, Carmine's brother Donato married Theresa's younger sister, Maria, so Carmine bought another two room house across the street. Teresa's mother, Maria De Luca, helped her move with a horse-drawn rental truck. The weather was cold and the street was muddy. Her granddaughter, Mary, had German measles and Maria De Luca prayed that if one of her granddaughters would die let it be Antoinette.

When they were in the new house, Antoinette did get the German measles and died at nine months of age.

On December 20, 1906, Carmine sold his little lot at 1271 Meade Street to the Realty Trust Company who bought the land for The Carnegie Steel Corporation's railroad tracks. Carmine received $3,000 for the land and thought he was a millionaire.

Carmine and his brother Donato decided to buy land in order to build houses. On February 20, 1906, they bought a large lot bordering Division Street, Waverly Ave and Argo Street. They paid $1100 to the Hawkins Farm Company of which Frank Hitchcock was president and David Tod secretary. There was a large hole on the land, so Carmine hired a surveyor to divide the land, leaving the hole on Donato's part. Donato didn't want the hole on his land either, so he got $25 cash and went downtown to hire his own engineer. Donato was mugged and robbed on the street and went back home. He built his home on the hill on Waverly Avenue and Carmine moved his home from Meade Street to 356 Division Street and added rooms to it. The brothers were estranged for quite a few years over the hole on Donato's property.

Carmine got a job at the Carnegie Works. There were two twelve hour shifts, 8:00 p.m. to 8:00 a.m. Carmine worked the night turn and made about $1.00 per day. The men worked 7 days a week, every day of the year, including Christmas. The conditions were bad and the men could not even stop to wipe their brows without their bosses hollering at them. Carmine was a hard worker and became a track foreman. He planted a large garden, made homemade wine with grapes grown in his grape arbor and was also the street lamp lighter.

Although Carmine made a fair living, he was tight

with his money. In 1919, he built a large store for Teresa in front of the house and added two bedrooms and a bath above. The children worked in the store. Mary made the bread, pizza, sausage and pepperoni, while Christine baked fancy pies and cakes. The children taught Teresa to read an write enough to take care of the store's business. They also taught her to play cards, which she enjoyed. After she gave Carmine his supper and he had left for the night shift in the mill, she would take her daughters next door to play cards with the neighbors.

Carmine, who was called *Frank*, got his father-in-law, Tony, a job in the Carnegie works. Anthony did not like to work and would use any excuse to stay home. It it was cold, he couldn't work because "I might get a chill;" if it rained, "I might get pneumonia;" and if it was hot, "I might have a stroke." He missed so much work, Frank's boss finally fired him. Frank had no use for his father-in-law because he was lazy.

Antonio was a big eater and loved to eat, especially eggs. He would go down the hill to his daughter Teresa's house, where she would prepare him a large meal of a half-dozen eggs, homemade bread, and sausage. Meanwhile, Frank, who worked nights, and should have been sleeping, would come downstairs and start yelling at Teresa for giving her lazy father all his food. They would yell and argue and Teresa would tell Frank that it was her food from her store and she could give it to her father if she wanted to. Frank would shout, "While he laid in his bed all night, I was in the mill working, and yet you give him all this food." Antonio, who believed in eating slowly and chewing every mouthful 30 times, would just keep on eating and chewing, his big eyes looking from Teresa to Frank, back and forth. Despite their fights, he always finished his meals and came back for more.

Teresa liked to sew and make clothes for herself and her family. One day an Arab peddler came down Division Street selling sewing machines. Teresa bought one for $30. She turned her back to the man and lifted her long skirts and petticoats to get the money from the top of her stocking. When Carmine found out how much the sewing machine cost, he wanted Teresa to return it to the peddler the next time he came by and get her $30 back. Although Carmine was very angry, Teresa kept the sewing machine.

When the children were older, the family would celebrate Carmine's name day in the Italian tradition. This was Our Lady of Mount Carmel Day on July 16. Carmine, who was not very religious, did go to church on that day dressed in his blue suit and red tie. When they returned from mass, they would invite the neighbors, family, and paisani to celebrate.

One neighbor would bring a concertina to play. Teresa would serve pizza she had made in the outdoor oven and lupini which she also made. They would have a cold keg of beer and Carmine's wine. They would dance the quadrille and the tarantella in the driveway to the concertina music. They had learned the dances in Italy. The quadrille is a dance done in groups of four like our American square dances, with a caller calling out moves.

In 1923, Carmine's eldest son William had surgery for a brain tumor in New York City. The surgery was successful but he died at age 20 of spinal meningitis. Carmine's brother Donato came down the hill to Carmine's home to make peace with his brother and offer his sympathies. The brothers cried and embraced and Donato went into the living room where his nephew was laid out. Donato reached into the casket to embrace his nephew when the lid came down hitting him hard on the head. The women who were in the living room cried out, afraid they would have another death. Donato was not injured and the brothers were friends until Donato died in 1927.

Teresa was very sickly and suffered from bowel obstruction. Her children did most of the house work, took care of the store and the younger children. Teresa was only able to do the cooking. While she was visiting her daughter Bridget in Gary, Indiana, she became very ill and died on August 13, 1931 of bowel cancer. Her young daughter Christine, had to accompany her mother's body home on the train for the funeral. The family was devastated and suffered greatly their mother's loss.

The people on Division Street were staunch Democrats and Mike Kirwin was one of their favorite politicians. Congressman Kirwin would hold rallies in my grandmother's store on Division Street. People would crowd in the store to hear his speeches. Mike referred to the Maino family as, *The salt of the Earth.*

After his wife's death, Carmine continued to live with his children. In July of 1933, his youngest son, Joseph (my father), was to marry Esther Rossi from Brier Hill. Esther's mother, Maria, was a poor widow and she approached Carmine for $30 or $40 to help out with the wedding. Carmine refused, saying he wasn't a millionaire. The day of the wedding, Carmine's son Mickey (Nicholas) drove Carmine, Sam, and Mary DePiore, Gerry, William and baby Eileen across the river to the wedding at St. Ann's. St. Anthony's had closed to consolidate with St. Ann's, but the Irish of that parish hated the Italians, so the diocese later reopened St. Anthony's. After the wedding, everyone went to the Rossi home on North

Avenue for the reception. Maria Rossi gave the Maino family sandwiches and wine and they left. When they were almost back to Division Street, Carmine said to his son, Mickey, "Go back Nicola, I forgot my hat." Mickey turned the car around and went back inside the house to get the hat. When he came out, he said, "You'll never believe what's going on in there. They have a table loaded with food -- wedding soup, meatballs and pasta, chicken, and salad!" I guess grandma Rossi figured if Carmine wouldn't help out with the wedding, she wouldn't put out food for his family.

I was born in December of 1935 when my grandfather was retired. I can remember him always wearing his work clothes and brown Romeo slippers. We would sit in the shade of his grape arbor and eat the sweet, purple grapes. Sometimes we would go down the cellar where he would get wine from the large wooden barrels there. Occasionally he would give me a sip from his little cut glass wineglass. He would also take me for walks in the woods where we would pick hazelnuts and put them in a burlap sack he brought. They weren't round like the one in the store, but oval. They are still my favorite nuts to this day.

Grandpa would take me to the store when he would cash his pension check. He carried a brown leather coin purse with 3 sections which he opened to get money to buy me a bag of penny candy. He would read stories to my cousin Eileen and me about Bartolo, a bandit in Italy who robbed the rich and gave to the poor. When Bartolo got captured, we would cry until he read us the next installment and Bartolo would escape. He also taught me to read the Sunday comics when I was four, and I am still an avid reader to this day, thanks to Grandpa.

Carmine would take his grandchildren for walks

on the Division Street bridge. He would put us up on the wooden railing and let us walk up there high above the railroad tracks. I can remember looking down at those large, round cars full of red hot molten steel. It was said if a man fell into one of these, they buried the whole car. Our mothers and the neighbors watched in horror and told Carmine not to let us walk up there, but he paid no attention.

When Carmine was 76, he took his granddaughter, Betty, to the barbershop on Salt Springs Road while he got a haircut. On the way down the Division Street hill, he fell on the sidewalk. Betty, who was only four, ran home to get help. Grandpa was put to bed and died of a stroke soon afterward on April 29, 1942.

Carmine and Teresa taught their children honesty, hard work, the value of an education and most of all, love and closeness of family. We are still a large, close, loving family and most of us do not live far from Division Street. Youngstown has changed a lot since Carmine and Teresa first settled here. The old wooden St. Anthony's Church has been replaced by a modern brick church. The old Division Street bridge with the wooden railing is gone, replaced by a modern expressway and new bridge. Busy freeways with speeding traffic cross the city. The mill is closed now, the smokestacks and blast furnaces no longer spew out fire, soot, and black smoke. The old white house is still there at the foot of the Division Street bridge. I would give anything I own to go back there for just one day, for the Feast Day of Our Lady of Mount Carmel and see my Grandma and Grandpa, when they were young, dancing the quadrille in the driveway of our old Division Street home.

Agnes Martinko

LEAVING THE FARM

In 1849, the 49ers went west for gold. The class of 1949 had some golden opportunity right here in Mahoning Valley. Jobs were plentiful but didn't always pay a lot of money. If you were able to get into the mill, though, you could get big money.

"Big" was the key word of the 50s. We had big cars, big ballrooms, and big bands to fill them. We drove those big cars to big screen outdoor movies and stopped at drive-in restaurants to get food on trays. And, in the case of my 1951 Nash, you could fold down the front seat and even sleep there.

Much of the steel to make those big cars was made in the big mills right here by the men making that big money. After the war, you didn't hear about any women working in the plants anymore. So, after graduation, I checked out the employment agencies and the want-ads to see what kind of big opportunity there would be for me.

One of the nuns at high school asked me if I was considering college. When I asked my father about that, he said that I already had about 10 years more schooling than he had in Europe and thought that I already had "college."

I didn't much care about college at that point so it didn't matter that I didn't go. Oh, my grades were o.k, but I didn't do real well except in subjects like Algebra or Geometry. You didn't have to study numbers. It was always so clear what you had to do. I don't know why the rest of the class had so much trouble.

It was the words that you had to study, especially the Latin and Spanish ones. I didn't have much time to study. All the students in the school boarded there and had supervised study every night. I was the only one who went home to the farm each day. Lots of time I had to walk the three miles back and forth. And, sometimes, if the hired man was gone on a binge, I had to milk the cows before I left. Once, I didn't change my shoes and brought a little of the barnyard into the classroom. It took a while before I noticed what everyone was whispering and laughing about.

But, I never let school or the farm interfere with my dancing. There was Jimmy Gunter's round and square dances at PointView, Benny Jones' big band at Yankee Lake, and all the polka bands at Avon Oaks. Not to mention all the dances at ethnic picnics at the Struthers pavilion and on portable dance floors everywhere. My sisters even rented one for a dance at the farm. Everyone used to tell me that I could polka before I could walk because my father used to hold me in his arms and dance with me as an infant.

All this dancing took money. The job I found was bookkeeper for a furniture store. The pay wasn't much but I liked to look at all the pretty furniture and the boss had a good looking-nephew that soon became my special friend. This was my first job after graduation, but not my first job. In fact, it seemed like I always worked. At least since I started carrying papers for the *Vindicator* when I was ten. And, there was always a lot to do on the farm.

Once I had a summer job at *Isaly's*. I worked 2 to 10, but the bus didn't get to New Bedford until midnight. I had about a mile to walk after the bus stop, along a dark country road. The dark never scared me. It was the lights. I could see the cars coming way off and always ran to the next driveway I came to and started toward the house. One time I couldn't quite make it. The car stopped and the men asked if I wanted a ride. I lied and said I lived at the next house. They went on.

I'll never forget my first day on that job. The person that hired me gave me a manual that had all the directions about how to make sundaes and sodas and I was to memorize all of it. I thought I had it all straight but there was a lot to remember. My first customer wanted a banana split. That really put me to the test! It was a scoop each of vanilla, chocolate, and strawberry ice cream. Then, you had to put chocolate syrup over the vanilla, pineapple over the chocolate, and strawberry over the strawberry. Next, you had to fizz out the whipped cream over the whole mess and be real careful 'cause it could shoot out all over the counter if you let it. The final touch was a maraschino cherry on top. It was so beautiful. I just wanted to stand there and look at it. When I finally put it on the counter in front of the customer, I had hoped he'd say, "It's too beautiful to eat." Instead, all he said was, "Where's the banana?"

I had lots of other jobs but I'll just tell you about

one other. That was at the Triangle Raincoat Factory. I was 14 but said I was 16 in order to get the job. I had never seen a sewing machine so big. And there was a huge room full of them. Do you know what makes a lapel lie flat against the chest? I never did either. That's what I had to do.

I'd turn the lapel to its back and start sewing a strip of bias tape where the crease was supposed to be. Then, I'd stamp the bias tape with a rubber stamp that had two lines on it, an inch apart. Next, I'd sew the rest of the crease, easing it into the tape so that when you were done, the inside of the crease was an inch shorter than the outside and it would flop over like it's supposed to.

This was great fun. It'd get so you never had to think about what you were doing. You'd just do it and let your mind go anywhere it wanted to go. Mostly mine just soaked up the conversations of the other sewers. Everyone talked real loud over the hum of the machines. They talked about everything. And I mean EVERYTHING! It was a real sew shop soap show.

After a training period, you were placed on piece work. That meant that instead of a salary, you would get paid for each piece you did. If you sewed real fast you could make more money than if you were on salary. I don't know if I went too fast trying to make more money or if I got too involved in the stories I was hearing, because one day, the supervisor came over with some of the coats that I had sewed and said my lapels weren't flopping like they were supposed to do. At the same time, she said she'd have to "let me go" because I wasn't as old as I said I was. I never knew if she would have kept me on in spite of my age if I had gotten my flops right.

But all those jobs before graduation never mattered. You only counted it as a real job if you were out of school. My job at the furniture store was a real job but it didn't last long. After a few months, my oldest brother came to see me at the store. I never saw him much. He was twenty-one years older than I was and left home when Mother got pregnant with me. Seems he was ashamed to have a little sister at his age. I think he wanted off the farm 'cause he and his buddy took off and went to see every state in the whole 48.

When he came to see me, he was working at Republic Steel along with my father and my other brother. He told me, in that know-it-all voice, that he was talking to some bosses at the mill and found out that they were hiring women that ran some new fandangoed type of a machine that would figure out how much steel was being made and be better at it than men adding it up in their heads.

I wasn't too interested 'cause I was just settling into the job I had. But then, he said he would pay the $100 tuition to go to this *Comptometer* School. You studied at your own pace there. He said it normally took 6 months but that if I finished sooner, I wouldn't have to pay him back the $100 and I could get a job that paid big money at any of the mills. This was an offer I couldn't refuse.

The "school" was on the 17th floor of the Mahoning Bank on the square in downtown Youngstown. The hardest part was making sure I didn't look out the window. I had never been so high in the sky before and it scared me to death. The next to worst situation was once when I climbed up the rafters of the barn almost up to where the hay fork was.

You see, what you'd do to store hay in the barn is to drive a wagonload of loose hay into the barn. Then, by a system of ropes and pulleys, you'd pull the fork down from the roof, jab the tines into the hay and lock them together. On the other end of the rope, a horse was harnessed to pull the rope. The rope lifted the hay to the barn roof and you pulled another little rope to release the lock and the hay fell where you wanted it. Mostly, it was my job to lead the horse to the stopping point that my father had marked. You had to be real careful to stop in time. If the horse went too far, it could tear the pulley off the roof. That happened once with me leading the horse, but only once.

I don't know why I climbed up to the barn roof that day. One of the neighbors went to get the hired hand to try to get me down. He told me to just jump on the hay. There was a lot of hay in the barn but it still looked a long way down. After awhile I could see there wasn't anything anybody could do, so I jumped. It wasn't so bad, but it never happened again.

I finished the comptometer course in three months. The owner would recruit new students at the nuns' school by saying, "and one of your alumnae completed the course in only three months!" I guess no one else ever did get through any sooner. I never told them about the $100.

The job (maybe I should say *position*, now) I got was at the Youngstown Sheet and Tube's Struthers Rod and Wire plant on Bridge Street. It was nice. It wasn't even like being "in a mill." The office was in a grey ranch-type house with a nice lawn and hedge around the lawn. It was like a green oasis, half way between the guard gate and the wire plant.

We were like a family. There was the Superintendent, Assistant Superintendent, his clerk, and a secretary on one side and three cost accountants and me on the other. The plant foreman for each shift would bring his tonnage times a predetermined cost factor for each coded type of rod, wire, or conduit pipe. It was a piece of cake.

The way the comptometer worked was like this. There were banks of keys representing the value from one to nine vertically placed in each of the ones, tens, hundreds, etc. columns. They were manually operated at first and you had to make sure you pressed the keys evenly so the correct amount would be calculated. You always cross checked your work so you'd know if there was an error.

There was another part to determining the cost of materials produced. That was the cost of all incoming materials. Those that came by rail had their papers forwarded to me. The truck driver, however, would pull up to the office and bring the paperwork to me. There weren't all that many and it was a nice diversion to take care of that task, too. All but one that is. In the fall, a local horse farm would deliver manure. This was used as insulation around the outside pipes so that they wouldn't freeze.

Sometimes the papers would be smeared with manure. The driver himself usually perfumed the room with his presence as well. It became the joke of the office when everyone recognized my displeasure. Sometimes, I'd see him coming and suddenly have to use the restroom, leaving one of the men to sign the papers. They'd say, "You're a farm girl. You should be used to this." They just didn't realize that that was the problem. I thought I had left the farm, or at least that part of it, behind me.

The day before Christmas was special. It would be my first office party. I arrived early with the goodies that would be shared later that day. As I opened the door I saw a large package on my desk, beautifully wrapped in pink aluminum foil. I didn't have to open it. One whiff told me what it was.

The assistant superintendent was the jokester. One day later on, on a warm sunny Friday, he was leaving to drive to his cottage at Conneaut Lake. He looked tired and said to me, "Agnes, I wish you could drive me there. I just don't feel like it." He died of a heart attack later that night at the cottage.

This was my closest experience with the death of a person. My mother died when I was two and a half. I do remember some things. Like the sweet smell drifting upstairs from the flowers around the casket in the living room. And looking out the window and seeing all the square top black cars weaving out the lane on their way to the church, looking like railroad cars with the hearse engine out in front. I remembered pictures and stories about my mother but it wasn't like working with a person every day and then suddenly, they weren't there anymore.

Things changed at the office. It wasn't just the new people. My comptometer was electric now and you didn't have to press the keys so hard. But, somehow, it took more effort than ever to get the job done. My furniture store boyfriend had gone off to be a state policeman. He left the store and tried for the big money in the mill but it didn't work out for him. The dirty jobs and 'round the clock shifts wasn't what he wanted to do for the rest of his life.

Even dancing sort of became old hat and I found myself starting to read a lot, something I never did very much. Oh, in the old grad school, there were a few beat-up ones the teachers would pass around, like *The Count of Monte Cristo* and *Ivanhoe*. In high school, I couldn't believe that there were so many books. My plan was to read all of them. But after four years, I only got up to Edna Ferber's *Cimmarron*.

One day, a friend said she knew a college student who needed people to practice giving Stanford Binet Individual Intelligence tests. I volunteered, not having a clue as to what it was about. It was absolutely fascinating! When the student said, "With an IQ like that you should be in college." I started reading more than ever, especially books about psychology.

When the state patrolman boyfriend came home for a visit we went to one of our favorite places, the *Airport Tavern*, for a drink and some serious conversation. It seems he got pretty friendly with a Howard Johnson waitress along the turnpike and wasn't sure if he loved her or still loved me. I told him don't worry, I was quitting my job, going to school in Pittsburgh.

The clerks in the personnel office couldn't believe I was quitting my job to go to school. They asked me, "What can you ever do that will pay you more than you get here?" They were right. After spending all of my savings getting an education, my first year teacher's contract was less than half of my salary at the mill.

But somehow, words were more exciting than numbers now. Worlds of ideas flew through my mind and my body got on planes that flew high into the sky, landed in places that I hadn't known existed. I think I've been to over a hundred countries at last count.

But, everything carries a price. I'm back home now. No, not at the farm. But, I can get there in fifteen minutes. The barn is still standing. Don't think those rotted beams will ever hold my weight again. The mills are gone, though. Oh, there's a few buildings and some rusted stacks but most got torn down and buried or carried away. But, in the country you can still catch the scent of new mown hay and dawn still brings another day.

Agnes K. White

LIFE DURING THE DEPRESSION (1929-1939)

Father was born in Connellsville, Pennsylvania. He came from a family of five, three boys and two girls. In those days people went back and forth to Europe, to their homelands by boat. My father was the only one born in the U.S.A.

In the early 1900's there was a flood in Johnstown, Pennsylvania and Dad's family lost all their possessions, even relatives, so they came to Youngstown and settled on the West Side near the Carnegie Steel Mill. My grandfather had a dry goods store. Also, he had a horse and buggy and he would go to the railroad station and pick up people coming from Europe with their trunks. He would help them find places to live.

In fact, four or five families would live together until they found jobs and went on their own. It so happened my grandfather on my mother's side was rooming in my father's house. He came to this country first, had left his family in Czechoslovakia until he saved enough money to bring them here. At that time my father was about twenty-three years old and single, so my grandfather said, "Oh, I have a daughter coming; she will just be the wife for you!"

My grandmother, my mother, and her three brothers arrived in October of 1913. They roomed at my father's house. By January, 1914 they were married. My mother was only sixteen years old and couldn't speak a word of English, only Slovak.

They made a beautiful couple. Their marriage lasted sixty-two years. I was the first born, in 1915. In 1917 my father bought three acres of land with a one-room log cabin on it. We lived there. Slowly, he remodeled the cabin and made it into a nice house where six more children were born. During the flu epidemic in 1918-1919, we lost a brother only nineteen months old.

My father worked in the steel mill and also did farming and raised chickens, cows, and pigs. We also had a horse that helped with the farming. In 1929, my father had a beautiful six-room house built next door. The log cabin was too small for all of us. In 1935, Mother had her eighth child, a girl.

I was the oldest in a family of eight. Since my mother couldn't speak English, she spoke to me in Slovak and that's all I knew. So, when I started school, it was very hard for me and I would cry and come home from school. My father, speaking the English language well, taught me at home. He had a slate and he would write words on it.

By the time I was nine years old, I knew the language well. In fact, I went shopping with my grandmother and interpreted for her! I had to do a lot of work at home. In those days, babies were born at home, delivered by mid-wives. I had to do all the housework, even milk cows.

My father had a horse and buggy; he took me with him everywhere. I remember when Father bought a Victrola, the wind-up kind. He would play records and pick up the babies and dance around the room.

We didn't have electricity. We had kerosene lamps. We had a coal stove in the middle of the room that heated the whole house. Clothes were washed on a washboard, hung outside. Father bought his first car, a Model-T, in 1926 for $600. We were so proud!

My childhood was different than kids today. We went everywhere with our parents. We didn't have telephones, radios, TVs. There was no *junk food*. An ice cream cone was a treat.

I started school when I was six. I went to kindergarten, then I went to a one-room school house for the first, second, and third grades. When I was nine years old, I went to a parochial school, where I graduated from the eighth grade at the age of fourteen. That was in 1929. I went to high school until I was sixteen and completed the tenth grade.

I got a job after tenth grade as a maid and went to part-time school one afternoon a week until I was eighteen. My first job, when I was fourteen, was a baby-sitting job paying five dollars a week. Then when I was sixteen, I left school and did the housework job for five dollars a week until I got married at nineteen. In 1948 I got a job in a bakery, where I worked for twenty-five years. I started at ninety-seven cents an hour and when I retired I was making $3.55 an hour.

The Depression is the reason I left school, because my father was out of work. What little bit I made I gave to Mom and Dad. The Depression started in 1929 when the stock market plunged way down. It was a curious kind of depression. The rich suffered first. They had the most money to lose. Anyone that had money in the bank lost it.

By 1930, men were out of work. People that had jobs took salary cuts. Hoover was president then. Soup kitchens opened up in cities. People would go with containers to get soup to feed their families. A bleak and wretched time, perhaps the lowest moments the country had ever known. Still, we lived through it.

I remember when Christmas came, there was no money to buy gifts. People would send things through catalogues which wouldn't arrive. We wore hand-me-down clothes. The schools gave out shoes. I used to walk with a friend about three miles to get day-old bread and cake and carry it home. That is when we went into the milk business. My mother milked the cows and bottled the milk, sold it for ten cents a quart.

People had very little money. Everyone stayed home and made friends, played cards. Then again people couldn't pay rent so families moved in with one another and shared. I remember one time we had three families living with us. We were afraid of losing our new home; all we could pay on the house payment was the interest. I could go on and on with the hard times we went through.

A typical day during my childhood was getting up to go to school. We dreaded that because it was about three miles away and we had no school busses. We either went with the baker or walked. If it rained or we had a heavy snowfall, we stayed home.

After we came home from school we all had

chores to do. My mother did all the farm work, so we had to do the housework. We never had bikes or skates to play with. We made up our own games.

Besides working in the mill, my father built three homes, helped in the garden, and cut grass to make hay for the cows. We went to the store for groceries every day since we had no refrigeration to keep foods from spoiling. On Sundays, we went to church. Maybe in the afternoon we would go to a show for ten cents or walk to Idora Park.

One important event I remember is I got married in 1934 and had my first-born in 1935, my second in 1936. We had very little money during the Depression. My husband worked on the WPA in 1935. By 1936 things were getting better. Then in 1938 came the blow. Abroad, World War II was brewing. Everybody was glued to their radios for news. Adolph Hitler was in charge. The United States got involved and the next thing we knew there was war. My two brothers had to go, one to Belgium, one to the Philippines. They were only eighteen years old. My poor mother cried constantly. My two brothers-in-law also went. But, thank God, they all made it home safe without any injuries.

SIT DOWN CHILD

Mary Thigpen Gibson

Arr. by K. Morris

Note: Sing 1st & 2nd Verse-then Chorus
3rd & 4th Verse-then Chorus
5th Verse-Chorus then Final ending

VERSE

1. He cried "moth-er what are you go-ing to do?" I said,
2. stop, look lis-ten too, I'm goin' to
3. roads are long the path-ways wide
4. mount'ns that seem so hard to climb on the
5. tell you there is al-ways a past

1-3 Go back to A for 2nd & 4th Verse

2-4-5

sit down child I'm goin' to pray for you. 2. You bet-ter
ask my God what can He can not hide. 4. The
sit down child be-cause you do for you.
oth-er side they bring you down a-gain.
slow down child be-cause you're run-ning too fast.

CHORUS

Now sit down, sit down, sit down, sit down,

Go back to A for 3rd & 5th Verse | Final ending only | Fine

sit down child I'm goin' to pray for you. 3. The pray for you.
5. Let me

60

DON'T FORGET ABOUT ME LORD

Arr. by
K. Morris

Words and Music by
MRS. MARY JANE THIGPEN GIBSON

Don't for-get a-bout me, Lord, Don't for-get your child,

Don't for-get a-bout me, Lord, You prom-ised peace af-ter-while.

Fine

1. Now your child is plead-ing on bend-ed knees, Your child is plead-ing, Please don't for-get a-bout me. 2. I've cried, "Lord, have mer-cy, have mer-cy on your child. I've pray'd for peace and con-tent-ment and rest af-ter-while.

Lucille Loury Stewart

I REMEMBER ST. ANN CHURCH

One of the earliest and most beautiful churches in Youngstown was the parish of St. Ann at the corner of Jefferson and West Federal Streets. It was spawned from St. Columba, the mother church of the valley. It was built of red brick and trimmed with sandstone, and modeled after the ancient churches of Europe. Its two towers rose heavenward and were visible from many parts of the city. The bells called many to Mass.

In 1869 the population of *Brier Hill* was growing. Bishop Rappe sent Rev. E. J. Murphy as the first resident pastor. Shortly after his arrival, Fr. Murphy purchased a lot on the corner of Federal and Calvin Streets for $1,000. A small frame building, formerly used as a store, was also purchased for an additional $100. Four parishioners, John Joyce, Michael Riley, Luke and Patrick Thornton, moved the building to the lot on Calvin Street. It was fitted up as a temporary place of worship and as a school.

Fr. Patrick McCaffrey became Pastor. He built the first church, a plain frame structure costing about $3,000. It was dedicated to St. Ann, the mother of our Blessed Mother and the Lord's grandmother.

I remember how large the church was and how beautiful the inside. Up the steps, passing through the large oak doorways of the vestibule, you were attracted to the main altar, which rose high into the graceful apse that enclosed the spacious sanctuary. The altar itself was highly polished oak carved with intricate, balanced design.

An elaborate statue of St. Ann rested in a high pointed niche, symmetrically offset by two other niches in which were statues of angels. The altar table was firmly braced by recessed pillars and a facing of inlaid panel work delicately carved. The entire altar, with its detailed pinnacles, impressive crucifix, and candle holders, rested upon three liturgically required steps, richly blue carpeted.

Two side altars, one for our Blessed Mother and one for St. Joseph, built in their customary places, were similar in design to the main altar.

A semi-circular passageway behind the sanctuary wall connected the priest's and altar servers' sacristy respectively. Large attractive doorways led from these sacristies to Shrine-altars of St. Ann, the Sacred Heart, St. Anthony, and the Little Flower of Jesus. Impressive stations of the cross vividly portrayed the Passion and Death of our Lord.

From the sanctuary and other details, our gaze anxiously followed up the slender recessed columns which, reaching to the uppermost point of the decade, terminated in a graceful arch to form the middle part of the church, the chief characteristic of the building. Springing from the middle part of the church proper, narrow, suppressed archways appeared as a series of gables, while stained glass panels arcaded the superstructure by their ribbed construction, as it was called. Massive walls admitted narrow, high, and fanciful stained glass windows which depicted figures of various saints. These richly patterned windows, receiving soft translucent rays of light which were easily diffused throughout the Church, were the colorful memorials of deceased parishioners.

The pews divided the floor plan into a spacious center aisle and two moderately wide side aisles. To the rear of the pew section kneeling angels resting on pedestals seemed to bid us to cleanse our hearts before entering the house of God.

Winding stairways ascended from each end of the high and neatly decorated vestibule, bringing us to the choir loft with ample space and a massive soothing-toned organ housed in its center. More diffuse light entered from slightly opaque upper windows, casting delicate, soft shadows and creating a sense of encouragement as it bathed a panoramic view of the church from the gallery. Interior decoration was in soft pastels, shades of blue and gray, and trimmed in gold. A pattern of blue stencil work covered the sanctuary walls, embellished in gold leaf. The high blue ceiling of the apse was studded with stars, which seemed to twinkle amid the rising vapor of burning incense at ceremonies. Gray-buff line coating in blue and silver detail gave the walls depth while pale blue nave completed the color scheme.

The following priests served as pastors at St. Ann's: Rev. F.J. Henry, Rev. Francis McGovern, Rev. John P. Barry, Rev. Thomas Walsh, Rev. Americo

Ciampichini, Rev. John Gilhooley, Rev. Achilles P. Ferreri, and Rev. William P. Dunn. Priests who served as assistant pastors include: Rev. G.E. Donnellon, Rev. F.T. Fergus, Rev. F.A. Cacciacarro, Rev. A.J. Winters, Rev. John Lenz, Rev. J.A. Flood, Rev. J.L. Brennan, Rev. Joseph Feicht, Rev. John Leteau, Rev. William Slipski, and Rev. John Lyons.

In 1892 Father Barry bought four lots at the corner of Federal and Jefferson Streets and the cornerstone was laid on July 17, 1906. In 1898 the old church was sold to the Italian Catholics, who organized that year under the patronage of Saint Anthony of Padua.

The first couple married in St. Ann's were Michael Golden and Margaret Mulherin, October 3, 1870.

St. Ann School, at the old location, was erected in 1872 and was placed in the charge of the Sisters of the Holy Humility of Mary. They were replaced in 1888 by the Ursuline Sisters. The new school, built with the church, was a four room structure with an enrollment of 250 pupils. Grades one through eight were taught by four Ursuline Nuns and one lay teacher.

The Altar and Rosary Society was organized during the pastorate of Father Barry, and was originally for women only. Later it was reorganized by Father Lenz to admit men as well. This idea was welcomed and fostered a society which enabled men and women to share in spiritual and social activity.

The main purpose was to provide necessities for the offering of the Holy Sacrifice of the Mass, such as altar breads, altar wine, candles, and linens. One of the most ardent workers this society has ever known, the late Miss Margaret Flemming, gave untiring effort to expand the society and accomplish good.

The St. Vincent DePaul Society was organized in

St. Ann Parish in 1940 to provide for the parish needy. It gave food and clothing to poor families and provided clothes for needy children in the Graduating, First Communion, and Confirmation classes. Baskets were sent to the poor at Christmas and school books were supplied to those who could not afford their own.

Square dances were held on Sunday evenings, sponsored by younger parishioners. The Confraternity of Christian Doctrine was a society made up of young people. It was their duty to instruct all Catholic children who were attending public schools in the fundamentals of the faith. Catechism classes were conducted from September until June after 8:30 Mass.

Boy Scout Troop #111 taught the boys of the parish to become upright citizens. The troop was proved outstanding, having received the highest camping grade at Camp Stambaugh in 1943.

The Circle Society of Women was organized by Father Ferreri to take care of the extra expenses of the rectory. The proceeds from their social functions purchased household linens, kitchen utensils, and other furnishings. Miss Florence Sharkey for many years worked preparing the sacristy altars and linens for ecclesiastical service, keeping everything in the church in order with the utmost care and solitude.

Many young men from the parish of St. Ann served their country during World War II. Four young men paid the supreme sacrifice of their lives: Clifford Hurst, Lawrence Galardi, Nicholas Fish, and Leo Nail.

On Sunday, October 29, 1944, more than a thousand people visited St. Ann Church to mark the 75th anniversary of the parish. A procession led by Bishop James McFadden opened the ceremonies with choir girls in new red gowns and altar servers. Dorothy Smith, a student of the school, gave the welcoming address. The bishop was presented with a bouquet. The bishop went to the church gallery to bless the new organ. A fifty-voice choir sang, accompanied by d'Nelle Riley at the organ. Rt. Rev. Msgr. Robert B. Navin, a native of the parish, reviewed the history of St. Ann's, with a particular emphasis on the thirty-four years of service given by Rev. John P. Barry. The bishop commented on the wonderful spirit of the parish, particularly commending the singing of liturgical music by the choir. Dinner was prepared by the altar guild and served by young women parishioners

I remember the beautiful Novena of St. Ann, which was held on her feast day, July 26. The church was decorated with flowers, linens, and many candles.

The Eucharistic Congress was held at Stambaugh Auditorium in June, 1936. As I was only in the first grade, I do not remember too much, but I do remember one thing which has always meant a lot to me. I won a large beautiful statue of St. Ann. Mom put the statue away in the closet with a sheet covering it so nothing would happen to it. One day Pastor Dunn stopped by to ask my mom if the church may borrow it for the Feast of St. Ann. Mom asked Father Dunn if he would give us a small statue; of course, he said yes. The church was happy and so was Mom.

I have that small statue in my home. You have probably seen the large statue many times at St. Ann's. When the church was to be destroyed, Father Dunn was transferred to St. Mary Parish in Warren, where the statue is to this day.

In 1936, I started grade school and began attending Mass at St. Ann's with Mom and my sister. The church was so big; the stained glass windows all around the church were just beautiful. In the fifth grade I was able to join the church choir. We had a lot of Latin to learn. At first it was hard, but as time went on I learned more and more songs. I loved the songs. At this time the Mass was said in Latin and the priest stood with his back to the congregation. We were required to attend daily Mass quite often during the school year.

All the first graders looked forward to a very important day, our First Communion day, which took place in May, 1937. The girls wore pretty white dresses and carried a white purse, where we kept our rosary beads, prayer book, and a scapular. I still have the white veil which I wore on my head.

The sisters always had beautiful pictures and art work on our bulletin boards. Sometimes we would stay after school and help wash the blackboards, so Sister could mark up the next day assignment.

In the month of May all the students would be in the procession to honor our Blessed Mother Mary. We made a live rosary. The girls wore a white dress and carried a red rose which was then placed in a vase near the Blessed Mother statue. The sisters taught us songs about Mary which we still sing in church today.

The procession for the midnight Mass on Christmas Eve was a lot of work practicing where Sister wanted us to go and learning all the music. It always ended up beautiful. The altar boys were always first, two acolytes and one server carrying the cross leading us up and down the aisles of the beautiful church. Then came the choir with our beautiful gowns that our moms had to get ready for us. Every year they were different in color and style, depending on which sister was in charge. A little first grader dressed as an angel carried the Christ child to the manger. Many Christmas trees added beauty to the church. All sizes of candles were placed on the altar.

The priests wore their special gold vestments.

As I grew older and studied more about my faith with my class, I was blessed by the Bishop at the sacrament of Confirmation in 1938. In June 1944, I graduated from the eighth grade and went on to Ursuline High School. There were ten boys and ten girls in our graduating class. I remained a member of the parish until I was married at the Church in 1954.

In 1960 the former St. Ann Church in Brier Hill disbanded when it was demolished to make way for the West Federal Street Expressway. Many of the parishioners still meet at periodical reunions. Although the building is gone, the memories and love of the parishioners will always remain.

Works Cited

Parish of St. Ann. *75th anniversary: St. Ann Church; Youngstown, Ohio; October 29, 1944.* Rev. H.E. Fabrizio, a member of the parish, authored the description of the church interior.

Leon Stennis. *Youngstown Vindicator.* Writes about one of the reunions.

Edith T. Hill

BELMONT BRANCH YWCA

Early in 1916, many of the thoughtful and caring residents of Youngstown were concerned about the cultural, social, and recreational training of African-American girls and young women. Dr. Hudnut, pastor of the First Presbyterian Church, on Wick avenue, brought it to the attention of the Y.W.C.A. Board Meeting on November 14, 1916, but no action was taken.

Then in 1917, a few women got together and talked with Miss Raphorn, Executive Secretary of the Central Y.W.C.A., trading ideas on how to organize a branch for African-American girls and women. From this conference a club of fifteen women was organized to study the assembly of an Association-- its purpose, its needs, and methods of raising money to finance such a branch. Within a year's time the club membership increased to 130. The club was named the

Preparatory Club and the following officers were elected: Mrs Queen V. Robinson, President; Miss Louise Connors, Secretary; and Mrs Josephine Finney, Treasurer. Although the members worked diligently, there was neither enough money nor members to organize a branch at that time.

These courageous women did not become discouraged. They continued with their efforts and on the 5th day of February 1918, in the basement of the Public Library, they met with the representatives of several African-American Clubs and church missionary societies and discussed plans to organize a colored community social center for women and girls.

Prior to this meeting, contact had been made with The City Community Service Society, an organization of white Youngstown businessmen who graciously offered to let them use a building on the corner of Belmont and Rayen Avenues. It was decided that the Center would be a subsidiary of the City Community Service Society.

Persons present at that meeting included:

Mrs. J.C. Ewing: Chairperson of the meeting
Mrs. J.M. Hanson: Chairperson of the City Community Service Society
Miss Estelle Steward: Secretary

Mrs. Anna Hadley
Mrs. Albert Buehrle
Mrs. Robert Docket
Mrs. George Westlake
Mrs. T.D. Berry-Price
Mrs. John Ogburn
Mrs. Andrew Johnson
Mrs. R.D. Lynch
Miss Rhoda Holmes
Mrs. Mary Lonesome
Mrs. Samuel Boggess
Mrs. J.H. Ragland
Mrs. Queen V. Robinson
Miss Isabel Cameron
Mrs. M.M. Morris
Mrs. Harvey Thomas
Mrs. H.P. Parker
Mrs. W.B. Brown

By April 1918, organization of the Colored Community Center was completed. The building at the corner of Belmont and Rayen Avenue was being repaired and furnished through the efforts of various clubs and interested individuals. Miss Ella Frazier of Pittsburgh, Pennsylvania, the first executive secretary, assumed her duties in March. Mrs. Ruth Mosley of New York was added as girls' work secretary.

On December 18, 1918 the building was opened to the public as the **Colored Community Center** with approximately 1,000 members. A vigorous eight day membership campaign produced 700 new members. Twenty-two girls were in residence. The first committee of management was chaired by,

    House Committee -- Mrs. J.V. Hansome
    Social Committee -- Miss Rhoda Holmes
    Industrial Committee -- Mrs. Andrew Johnson
    Religious Committee -- Mrs. John Conrad
    Finance Committee -- Mrs. Albert Buehrle
    Education Committee -- Miss M. Estelle Stewart
    Membership Committee -- Mrs. J.H. Ragland

The center hummed with activity. Since the First World War was in progress, in addition to the normal activity, there was a Red Cross Unit organized by Mrs. Fred Orr with 100 Senior members and 30 juniors. Miss M. Estelle Stewart served as chairperson.

Two years after those thoughtful women founded the *Preparatory Club*, their goal was in sight. On April 8, 1919 the Executive Committee of the City Community Service Society met with the Y.W.C.A. and was opened to the public.

A May 1921 letter from the surviving members of the Community Welfare Committee-- Robert Bentley, James A. Campbell, J.G. Butler, Jr. and Henry Garlic (who controlled the Belmont Branch property) stated that the property would be transferred to the Y.W.C.A.

with the stipulation that it would be kept in good repair and would be used only for Association purposes. Transfer was accomplished by resolution and the Y.W.C.A. Board accepted the property under the stated conditions. The Colored Committee accepted the Resolution and agreed to pay the Y.W.C.A. $2,000 to be used for improvement of the Belmont Avenue property.

The following ladies were recorded as founders of the Belmont Branch Y.W.C.A.:

Mrs. Harry Biass
Mrs. J.C. Ewing
Mrs. Queen Robinson
Mrs. W.B. Brown
Mrs. R.D. Lynch
Mrs. Ella Smith
Mrs. Mary Exum
Mrs. Hannah Boggess-Price

Mrs. Henry Potter
Miss Estelle Stewart
Mrs. John Green
Mrs. Irene Stewart
Mrs. Thomas Callens
Mrs. C.C. Lottier
Mrs. Nonie Berry-Price
Mrs. Harvey Thomas
Mrs. Clara Winston

Miss Ella Frazier continued on as Executive Secretary, becoming the first Executive Secretary of The Belmont Branch Y.W.C.A. After three years service with both organizations-- the Community Center and Belmont Y.W.C.A.-- Miss Frazier resigned to serve as Executive Secretary of the Harrisburg, Pennsylvania Branch Y.W.C.A. She returned to Youngstown as guest speaker at the May 1945 membership Tea.

Miss Anna Hope of Atlanta, Georgia became the Executive Secretary in 1922, and Miss Margaret Moore became the Girl Reserve Secretary in 1923.

It was not until November 20, 1923 that the Central Y Board voted that in accordance with the constitution, a committee on *Colored Work* be appointed. They also approved the appointment of a colored chairperson, Mrs. Daniel Lynch, for the Committee of Management of the Belmont Branch.

During the organizing time many activities were in process at The Belmont Branch Y.W.C.A. As a community house, staff and diligent volunteers were striving to cater to as many persons as possible in the community. By 1930 there was a pre-school class for children, and school-girls were participating in Girl Reserve activities. The Phyllis Wheatley and Dunbar Clubs had been established for older girls and the professional women had organized the El Progresso Club, directed by Mary Alyce Florence.

Belmont Y annual events included a "cheer party" at Christmas time for the elderly and handicapped. Transportation was provided. A membership dinner meeting with a guest speaker of prominence was held every year. Sara Rouse Bachelor, who was membership chairman in 1942, set a goal of 1,000 new members. Evidently she reached her goal. Records show a membership of 1,251 in January of 1943.

A concert each year was the special event for the general Education Committee. Under the leadership of Mary Lovett-Belton the committee brought community concerts raising Youngstown's culture awareness.

Girl Reserves observed a very special event at their all-day conference, an annual event for them. An article in the December 2, 1933 edition of the *Youngstown Vindicator* features Mrs. George Alderdice, President of the Central Y, complimenting the Belmont Y for offering "unexcelled opportunities for service.... serves colored girls and women....a Community Center for colored people." Mrs. Alderdice described the activities of the clubs and told of other activities, such as a basketball league of eight teams with 60 girls and women participating, the games being played at the

West Federal Street Branch Y.M.C.A. A Red Cross sewing class of eighty women met three days a week. Lunch was served by the work committee. The group completed 3,400 garments. The Triangle Mother's Club had an enrollment of 57 mothers of school girls who met to study family problems and sex education. Book review meetings were held monthly to examine books written by and about Blacks. Interest in Black authors and Black Literature was stimulated.

Mrs. Alderice also spoke of the Junior Matrons, a group of young married women; The Glee Club; The Dramatic Club; and also a young people's Lyceum. Speakers were asked to discuss timely topics for 45 minutes with 20 minutes devoted to an open forum. The 1930's and 40's were the most active years at Belmont. During the 33 years the Belmont Y was in existence there were 11 Executive Secretaries and 12 Girl's Work Secretaries. Alice Warner Parham served the longest as Executive. Margaret Moore-Smith served the longest as Girl's Work Secretary.

In October of 1950 an objective study of the existing programs was done by Mamie Davis to determine what was the place of the Belmont Branch within the total Y Association. This marked the beginning of the consolidation of the Branch with the Central Y.

In advising its members how to make the transition, the Central Committee requested that they encourage Negro women and girls to enroll in their programs and see to it that when they did they had a pleasant experience. Also, they were directed to work toward assigning program responsibilities to staff without considering the race of staff members.

Belmont Branch Y.W.C.A. was dissolved on January 31, 1953. The Belmont Building was sold to the Thornton laundry on May 2, 1955.

Valerie Esker

TO WEST-SIDE JIM

I remember the meadow down Hazelwood
where we once played tag on the hill.
I can still hear the far-away whistle blow
where our daddies worked hard at the mill.

I see visions of tall wild-flower grasses,
windy acres of white Queen Anne's Lace.
When summer's coming suspended school classes,
quick to the meadows we'd race.

Now ripe wild-berry hunts fill my day-dreams;
they once filled my mouth with sweet bliss.
Old memories grow more poignant it seems...
remember our first meadow kiss?

Pat McKinney

GHOSTS

When I was in first grade at Sacred Heart School in 1963, our classroom was on the top floor of a building set on top of a hill. The entire south wall, save a window seat, was of glass and was close enough to fill the whole window with a big, brown, busy burning steel mill. I found it most enchanting.

During recess my friends and I clung to the chain link fence. We wondered if our fathers who worked in the mill could see us watching them. We waved, just in case, and discussed the things we saw in the smokes of many colors rising from the stacks. Poodles, whales, old men's faces, and women with puffy hair-do's. Many a magic dragon I saw rising above dark castles. From a stack in the middle there climbed a blue pillar of fire one hundred and twenty feet into the air. Trains and cranes moved about. Music was a heavy chain drawn through a pulley. Little lights flashed. Many kinds of whistles, each with a pattern and meaning of its own, tooted. Periodic explosions rumbled. Beautiful pigeons floated through it all. The heavy metal rumblings of giant engines boasted. I stood transfixed.

In autumn, the odor of sulphur mixed with the ghosts of many trees. In golden cold winter mornings the smoke swathed the dark forms in a halo and little whirlwinds of glittering graphite arose in the corners of the limestone buildings ... as if conjured up.

Ghosts.

Jean Dalrymple Deibel

BANCROFT SCHOOL

It is a majestic building of mellowed brick that stands grandly on the corner of Wychwood Lane and Southern Boulevard. It was following the Great Depression that diminutive principal Miss Amy Eldridge ruled here with an iron hand. Here was the place where we marched in line, *never* put our mouths directly on the water fountain and pledged allegiance each morning. Taskmaster Miss Grubb drilled us on the multiplication tables, and Miss Riley made sure we could diagram a sentence. The in-residence dream boat, Norman Paulin, had his name in hearts on all the girls' notebooks while his counterpart, Joyce O'Malley, black curls caught with satin ribbons, had admirers in most every grade. It was on the playground that dodge ball separated the meek from the mighty. More timid souls jumped rope or played jacks. In winter, dressed to the teeth in zippered snow suits with matching mittens and hoods, we trekked home at noon for a quick fix of Campbell's tomato soup. Time seemed to march on forever in a procession of Christmas vacations, Halloween costume parties, and Valentine boxes. In this insular world we were safe and sound. Nothing bad could happen there. We were a mixed bag of different backgrounds, a microcosm of Youngstown in the late thirties and early forties. We were the children of doctors and lawyers, steelworkers and storekeepers, barbers and carpenters. Mothers in house-dresses stayed home and tended the flock. More than likely a grandparent was part of the household. Often a second language was spoken at home. We thought nothing of it. Still, if I look over my shoulder, I can see Miss Duncan and Miss Arthur, eyes peeled for any transgressors, patrolling the halls. I can smell the intoxicating scent of oiled chalkboards and disinfecting cleaner, a tart sweetness that burns the nose. Today old Bancroft School is alive with the voices of children. Still a beacon on the far South Side, a kind of fortress, it seems as if nothing bad will ever happen there.

Charles Curry

WESTSIDE MEMORIES

First, the neighborhood around 4098 Burkey Road. There were still great stands of trees all around; a country store that probably was a holdover from before the houses went up, with their large backyards; there was even a farm up the road from our corner, hidden by a stream of trees. I have a vague memory of going with other kids to play in the barn there, and I think the proprietor had a pet monkey, and he never allowed us up into the barn loft. I told this story once to a fellow passenger on a train and, at this point, he jumped to a logical conclusion about that barn loft. Maybe you have also; but in any case, the end of this story is the police parading down our street one evening to raid the farm and close down the gambling casino in the barn loft.

Tell you the truth, though, I don't know any longer how much of this is memory and how much was told to me after the fact.

This was in Austintown. It was just up the street -- the corner where my family lived -- from a busy crossroads with stores, traffic, and Immaculate Heart of Mary School, but all that was out of sight of our corner. The neighborhood as I remember it was modestly heterodox; I remember an elderly English couple living nearby, and at one point a family of Chinese immigrants moved in. But, again, the truth is that neither of these neighbor families made much of a part of my young life. I remember more clearly a fire in the screen of trees between us and the farm; and I remember the day we didn't go to Idora Park.

Like a lot of others, our family passed a great deal of time in Idora Park. My own favorite was the Tilt-A-Whirl ride, and on one day in particular my head was so full of memory-pictures and anticipations of the Park that I got away from my parents, running madly ahead, not seeing much of anything around me. My parents soon called me back. We had inadvertently come on what was considered then as "colored people's day."

The thing, however, that made the earliest and most vivid impression on me, I think, was going to Vindicator Square one day in the 1950s with my parents. I think it might have been a cold day, and I remember the Vindicator building with plate glass windows on one side, where you could see large stacks of newspapers piled up inside the lobby. There were men standing around near the windows, not as I remember it in a line, but randomly, not carrying signs of any kind. It was plain to me, by one means or another, that anyone who wanted a newspaper could simply go into the building and pick one up. My parents went home without a paper.

Whatever moved my parents' reluctance to go into that lobby during the delivery strike, and they were not very much engaged in politics -- they are Democrats, I think, as much from habit as from conviction -- I have learned from them that politics is as much about sticking to a set of principles as it is about office-seeking. That day on Vindicator Square, I believe, was the beginning of my education.

Carol Miller

IT'S THE FRAGRANCE THAT MAKES A NEIGHBORLYHOOD

People from all over the neighborhood came when they smelled Baba Soby's homemade "pankuski," donuts fried in lard, covered with sugar. Homemade donuts loaded with fat, sugar, cholesterol, and taste.

She was not Baba Soby to me, just Baba, my grandmother. Baba means grandmother in Slovak. The whole neighborhood called her Baba Soby, even other babas who were her own age. She loved being called Baba; she loved all who called her that. She had fire in her soul that reflected glowing personality.

Baba lived well. She was a poor woman rich in blessings. However, like many immigrants who settled in our area, she knew hard times. She spoke of the loss of her children, the house lost during the Depression, and the love of family and friends who saw her through tough times.

I was blessed, as well. I was Baba's sounding board for many years. My parents both worked and my sisters were old enough to go to school. I was the (unspoiled) baby of the family. We lived next door to my grandparents and they were my baby sitters for many years. They were well seasoned, too. They had eleven children. A son and a set of triplets were deceased; still, their remaining seven children bore twenty-three grandchildren. Before her death, Baba witnessed also the birth of five great-grandchildren. Each new birth brought inner joy; she bestowed upon them Slovak blessing -- peace, happiness, longevity.

My grandparents had twenty-three grandchildren whom they probably loved equally. Yet, in my heart I was convinced I was their favorite! We spent much time together before I started school and during summer vacations until my teens, when I began to work.

Like most of the neighbors their age, my grandparents never learned to drive. They walked just about everywhere they went, and if it was too far to walk, they rode the bus. For Baba and me, the bus was a magic carpet that took us to wondrous places. We stood at the corner of our street, waiting for the carpet to arrive. During that time, she talked about how the neighborhood had changed over the years. When she first moved there, only two other houses were on the block. The school and church across the street were not built until much later. She talked about chickens, ducks, and rabbits in her yard and the escapades of raising, slaughtering, and cooking them. It was fascinating. I was so enthralled with the stories that I was secretly unhappy to see the bus come. I knew the stories would be carried away in a cloud of diesel exhaust.

Our magic carpet took us many places. We went

uptown to shop at Murphy's, Sears, and Stambaugh's. We ate lunch at Wheeler's restaurant. Uptown was an enjoyable shopping trip. Still, my favorite place to go was downtown. We shopped at McKelvey's collecting green stamps, Grant's, Lerner's, Livingston's, and Strouss's. I liked Strouss's best. We shopped in the basement where all the bargains were. We always ate lunch there, in the basement of Strouss's. There were no chairs. We stood at the counter to eat. I always had a hot dog, with a grilled bun that looked more like folded bread than a bun, and Baba always had a grilled cheese sandwich. The hot dog was good, but I always ate really fast, because I could not wait for dessert. We always had chocolate malts. They were the best I have ever had. The malts were the pot of gold at the end of the magic carpet rainbow ride.

Traveling about the city on our magic carpet was fun. Baba pointed out different sights during our journey. She talked about churches and schools we passed, some neighborhoods she used to live in, and the ethnic groups of people who settled in some of those areas. She would tell me about the happy times she had in the city she loved. She was a wonderful tour guide; even strangers sitting around us were not strangers long, they too joining in the discussions.

The bus trips were infrequent, saved for special sales or special needs. Most of the time, we stayed home. There, Baba cooked, sewed, crocheted, and made flowers. My grandfather, Czedo in Slovak, usually sat in the living room looking out the window. When I close my eyes, I can still see him in his old rocker in front of his radio that stood at least three feet tall. I still hear the squeak of the chair and the voice on the radio, "This is Paul Harvey, good day."

My grandparent's prearranged marriage lasted a

long time, fifty years until my grandfather died. He was a rather unpleasant man most of the time. My neighborhood friends feared him because he would always yell at them and tell them to go home. Baba would call them back over and tell them not to worry about him. When we talked about him and their marriage, Baba would say, "Husbands are all alike; put them into a paper bag, shake them up, and pull out any one; it would not make any difference." That was how their life was. They learned to live together at home and with their neighbors, putting up with each other's faults without fighting too much or divorcing.

Even when we did not summon the magic carpet, we still went on outings. Often, we would walk to the Shady Run Swimming Pool. Of course Baba would not swim. She just stood outside the fence and watched. As she watched, she chatted with other neighborhood friends who were also spectators. Our hot summer nights were spent at Pemberton Ball Field where we enjoyed the baseball games. Baba knew just about everyone there. If she did not know someone in the crowd when we came, they were old friends by the time we were leaving. Sometimes the neighborhood kids would play baseball in one of the larger lots on the street. Once we convinced Baba to take a couple of swings. She even made it to second base! We all told her she was a good baseball player. She just chuckled and said, "Oh, you so silly!"

Baba was famous in the neighborhood for her pankuski, but she was famous in Lansingville for her flowers. She made beautiful flowers out of ribbons and would arrange them in baskets for anniversaries and special parties. On our excursions to Grant's she would buy green tape, wires, and little decorations to put into the arrangements.

During her flower making, Baba gave me my first recycling lesson. She was friends with Mr. Yuhasz, the local funeral director. For her, he saved all the ribbons that came on funeral baskets. We took the ribbons home, removed the words *son* or *mother*, and wound them into spools. Baba carefully ironed the ribbons and cut them into the shapes she needed for her flowers. People always raved about Baba's baskets and were honored to get them as gifts. She even sold them to various people who in turn gave them as gifts. They were beautiful. However, as I grew older, silk flowers became the rage, and for whatever reason, I never learned how to make her famous flowers.

Now that I think about it, I never really learned how to make any of the things for which Baba became so well known. Besides her pankuski and flower baskets, Baba crocheted beautiful afghans and baby clothes. My lack of learning certainly did not stem from a lack of appreciation for what she did. I did recognize and appreciate her and her achievements while she was living. Now, seventeen years after her death, I mourn the fact that I did not learn those skills from the best craftsperson I have ever known.

Why didn't I learn them? I guess it's because Baba was so comfortable with her talents that she took it for granted that all others were comfortable in their attempts. Perhaps it was because she lived her whole life in an era filled with simplicity. Even as the decades passed, she never journeyed into the present. I remember once someone bought her a pair of pants so that she could go to a football game without freezing. Baba said that she could never be seen in public without a dress, and she wasn't. She went to the game wearing a dress with new pants underneath!

Baba followed no recipes for anything. She had

no patterns or written directions for baby sweaters. She just crocheted them. Once I asked her to teach me to make pankuski. She started with a big pot and in it she placed two eggs, some sugar, and flour. I asked, trying to write out the recipe, how much flour and sugar? Baba replied, "Add a couple handfuls of sugar, enough flour to make the dough feel right." What is a handful and when does it feel right? Baba said "Take it easy, you'll know when it's right."

That was how she and the neighbors around us lived; they took it easy; they knew it was right. They did a good bit of their shopping at Connie's, the corner grocery store. (Oh, my, I am becoming like her, just how much is a "good bit" anyway?) They filled prescriptions and bought cards at Peremskie's corner pharmacy. They grew and canned their own vegetables, baked their own bread, and slaughtered their own chickens. They were happy, and the neighborhoods were one big extended family. Nothing went on in the neighborhood that everyone did not know about and everyone did not participate in. When there were weddings, everyone baked cookies, everyone shared in each other's tragedies, graduations, births, or deaths, bringing food and heartfelt friendship.

It was a simpler time then. We need more of that era now. As I sit here typing, the neighbor's security alarm is sounding for the third time today. This neighborhood, a suburb of Youngstown, is new to me; I have been here only six months. The alarm is sounding from a home whose owners I have never met. In Baba's day, the neighbors would have greeted new neighbors with pankuski or pies. Everyone would meet the new neighbors by the end of the first week. If I could just fill the air with the smell of pankuski, my new neighbors would come running!

Madelyn T. Sell

GRANDPA'S HOUSE

    In the dead heat of summer we slept on the narrow porch of our grandparents' house on the East Side of Youngstown. It was a large frame white two-story house with a hilly front yard and gravel driveway which led back to the garden and chicken coop. I can remember being excited about sleeping over one summer night. But the newspaper came and the headlines were sad. St. Columba Cathedral burned down. Mom cried. Grandpa cried. They were devout Catholics. Nevertheless, we got to sleep on the porch that night.
    Other times, when it was not so warm, we slept over in one of the upstairs bedrooms. There were three large ones. One, the master bedroom, had a huge brass bed. Off the bedroom was a small room which housed a most interesting item -- a trunk! It was a battered thing that no one could open unless Grandpa was in the room. He would open it and take things out. The trunk held memories of the past. It was brought from Italy via Ellis Island many years back. The trunk was mysterious because there were so many strange things in it. We weren't allowed to touch it. Once in a while Grandpa would take something out and tell us the story behind it. Recently, I visited Ellis Island, saw trunks like Grandpa's.

Being devout Catholics, my grandparents had many statues scattered all around their house. In particular, I recall the statue of the Sacred Heart. There were several of these. My grandparents belonged to Sacred Heart Church on the East Side. The large Sacred Heart statue made me nervous. The eyes always seemed to be watching, just like the eyes of the Mona Lisa. On the landing of the second floor, there was a "shrine." Several statues were grouped, with votive candles placed all around. My favorite was St. Theresa, my patron saint, for whom I was given my Confirmation name. Over the years, I remember many scary, thunderous storms. I was grateful for those votive candles. They helped to make things less frightful for this six year old.

Staying overnight meant taking walks in the neighborhood. It was safe to walk anywhere. I particularly loved walking to Bootsie's store on the corner of Truesdale and Shehy. Bootsie had big glass shelves with tons of penny candy. For a dime, one could get a big brown bag full of candy. My favorites were Black Jacks and Mary Janes. He always threw extra pieces in too, because he liked my grandpa.

Down the other end of the street was Rupp's Dairy. Mr. and Mrs. Rupp were nice people, but a kid couldn't touch anything. You had to be with an adult, even in those days. They had Nehi beverages there. I liked root beer and lime.

Occasionally, if Grandpa felt up to it, we would board a city bus to the Sharon line. This is where Grandpa had his "secret garden." I don't really know who gave him the o.k., but he cultivated a huge garden of peppers, tomatoes, garlic, and other vegetables on this huge piece of property. This took the whole day, but it was a great adventure. We brought back vegetables and fruits for the whole neighborhood!

Grandpa did work for a living, too. He worked at Republic Steel. Sometimes he worked night shifts. When this was the case, we had to be quiet during the day when he slept. Absolutely no noise, at all! Grandma would be busy in the kitchen baking bread and corn fritters, her specialty, and getting his big black lunchbox packed full of goodies. Grandpa worked hard and had little time for relaxation.

Another "job" he had was slaughtering the turkey for Thanksgiving dinner. I recall once when he dragged a live turkey down the cellar and got an ax, and chopped the head off! I watched it! It was definitely violent!

The cellar was a story in itself. I was particularly curious about the big coal furnace. It was like an octopus with all those tubes. Grandpa would open the door to the furnace to shovel the coal in and all I could think of was, "If that's what hell looks like, I'm gonna start being real good!" The cellar had another niche. In a corner of the other end of the cellar was this tiny room. One had to reach in to feel for the light cord. It was dark and damp. Now I picture a scene from Poe's *A Cask of Amontillado*. This small room housed homemade wine. The bottles had labels affixed. Each bottle was dated. This had no meaning for me then. It does now. I wish I had stolen a bottle for a keepsake.

Three years ago, while on the East Side of Youngstown, I drove past Grandpa's house on Shehy Street. It was painted an ugly blue. The yard was overgrown with weeds and the neighborhood was run-down. I drove down the street quickly. I was depressed. When I got home that day, I erased the picture of the old house from my mind. I wanted only to cherish the memories of the Grandpa's house I once knew.

Theresa Moon

JUST TO BREATHE

    The heat of the day does not fade with setting of the sun; it dips a bit to acknowledge the lack of light, but doesn't loosen its grip on the living by more than a degree or two. We come out from behind the shade of closed doors and drawn drapes to gather in communal misery on the porches of the neighborhood. Muted greetings and half-hearted rumblings about the heat are exchanged as we take to our porches in search of an elusive cool breeze. A sticky stillness hangs in the humid air, making it an effort just to breathe.
    Eventually it grows quiet and the dogs, spooked by a passing car, begin their night song. It's a concert now, they seem to outnumber the people on our street. Not to go unnoticed, the few feline residents of our corner of the city make themselves apparent by the glow of their eyes and the whoosh of their tails as they dart across the street fresh on the hunt.

The steady stream of daily traffic on Salt Springs Road has begun to thin out and on my street, Elberen, the pace slows as well. The light of the moon and the quiet rhythm of the evening leads my thoughts back into the past. As if in a dream I can see the people who lived here not so long ago. Images flit through my mind, picture postcards of a collective past: the mill with its workers, their families, their homes, their churches and clubs. Nighttime and the stillness combine to make these images dance through my heat-scorched mind.

The mill and its buildings are gone now, torn down in an effort to forget the past and get on with the future. My school bus used to pass that square brick building next to the tracks where Steel Street and Salt Springs Road converge; I used to watch the men in denim and flannel cross the walkway under the union sign that kept track of hours without accidents. I remember the old-timers who cried when the building came down. Then I couldn't fathom their tears for a simple building; now I realize that it was the pain of forgetting that trickled down their lined faces. I cannot forget them; the history of these few streets calls to me in a voice best heard in the poetry of darkness.

Across Salt Springs Road sits Cherol's grocery store and banquet hall. The store's pressed metal ceiling is adorned in an ornately detailed geometric pattern that's hard to find these days. Next door the banquet hall stands, its old-style glass block topped off with aged red neon glamour. Its glory days belong to the past, a time when the big bands played on Saturday nights, when ladies wore seamed stockings and gentlemen wore hats. I've been inside and seen the undersea sculptures along the walls and tremendous plaster clamshell backdrop on the stage. I can almost hear the clarinets in the cricket song and see the glitter of rhinestones in the lights of passing cars.

Up the road on Belle Vista sits Saints Peter and Paul's Church. What a grand church it is -- Orthodox, with a Russian minaret roofline covered in oxidized copper shingles. When I close my eyes I can see the cycle of life inside its walls: hope-filled baptisms, lifetime marriages, somber deaths, an endless loop of one life after another complete in its own design. The emotions of life echo through curving spires, resonate in the music of the bells that still play each Sunday.

Time moves on and people move in and out of our lives, yet the places where our lives unfold seem to remain, stand as storehouses of our collective memories. These places promote a sense of continuity. Even now people gather at Cherol's banquet hall to celebrate life's joys. The parishioners work diligently to keep Saints Peter and Paul beautiful. The mill is gone, but its memories are not likely to fade.

The heated darkness no longer seems oppressive; rather, it has a quality of comfort, an amiable awareness of friends close by, separated only by time and memory. The past that intrudes into my thoughts begins at last to fade into the scrapbook of my tired mind, the moonlight grows bright in the fullness of the evening. The dogs are quiet and the cats have retired. My mind is at peace now and it's time to let this day take its place among the postcards of the past.

Joyce Farrell

THE LOVE AFFAIR

It started so long ago that I can't remember when I first fell in love, but once it set in, nothing could change how I felt, and certainly no one could change how I felt, and still feel. I first met my lover when I was a young girl of ten, and it was love at first sight.

Before anyone gets the wrong idea, my one true love is a city, specifically Youngstown, or at least the Youngstown I first met on that July day in 1950, when my grandmother and I went to town for the first time.

I had moved here from a small town in Pennsylvania, and the thrill of seeing a **big city** was more than I could stand. As the bus neared the Square, and I saw the Central Tower for the first time, I just knew that I had to explore every floor.

Grandpa would tell me about the city, and told me that there were certain places that a little girl just never went to, so, true to my adventurous heart, I made notes. Before school started I was determined to explore downtown Youngstown until I knew it like the back of my hand, and explore it I did.

Most people today have long forgotten what a wondrous place the downtown of the '50s was, but etched into my heart is a complete picture of it, and as I go to work each day, in my mind's eye, the present downtown is replaced by the images that I saw that first year. Not a building, not a store, not an alley escaped my prying eyes; everything and everyone was fair game.

The *East End* from the Square to the Elephant Bridge was considered "no-man's land" to the respectable folks in the neighborhood. They would send their maids there to shop for all the bargains, but few would go there themselves. Well I went.....and I'm here to tell you that it was a wondrous sight.

You may have heard stories about the gambling joints that were located on the East End....the Greek Coffee Houses where in back rooms men gambled hundreds of dollars, and ice cream parlors that were fronts for the numbers racket. Yes, I even explored those places, and I am proud to say I developed a fondness for Greek food. On the corner of Watt and Boardman was located a confectionery store that I passed several times before ever going in, but one day I did, not knowing that it was the central drop for the numbers.

You can imagine the surprise in the owner's eyes when an eleven year old girl came in and ordered a dish of ice cream. You can also imagine the consternation in the hearts of the numbers runners who had to wait until the man got me that dish of real homemade ice cream made with real cream.

The next place I stopped at was one of those

Greek Coffee Houses. I couldn't understand why the place was empty when the street was bustling with people. As I walked in, an old man looked up from his paper, and asked me what I wanted. Obviously, I wasn't there to gamble my allowance away. I walked over to a showcase that was home to a vast array of Greek pastries, and asked what I could buy for a quarter.

Now mind you, those pastries were only for show, and the shop was not intended for little girls, but the man, realizing that I had no idea what the true nature of the place was, selected several pastries, and telling me to sit at the table, brought them over with a huge glass of cold milk. When I went to pay him, he just laughed and said that it was his treat.

Another favorite stop was a newsstand on Boardman street right across from the Ohio Edison building. To the unaware, it was just that, a newsstand that sold newspapers from far away places, but to those who knew better, it was a horse-betting joint.

In time, I covered just about every place that I was told to stay away from, and I must say that as I got to know the people, and the people got to know me, I made a great many friends.

In time a ritual developed. First, every Saturday, when I would go to one of the movies, my first stop would be the confectionery store for a dish of ice cream, then to the Greek Coffee House for a bag of cookies, then, armed with these treats I'd head for the show. The Palace, the Paramount, the State, the Warner, or the Strand!

As I entered my teens, like others my age, the favorite spots to go to were the record departments of McKelvey's and Strouss Hershberg's. Each had booths where a person could listen to records before buying them. Then there was Sinkwitch's Restaurant. If we were really lucky, we might get to see Frank, the Chaney All-Star football hero turned pro. Every Saturday morning we would head over to the Record Rondezvue where Dan Ryan held court.

Back in those days we could, if we were lucky, get a chance to get into the studios of WFMJ radio for a live show that featured one of the nation's big bands that were appearing at The Elms or Idora Park. Or, if we were lucky, we could save up our allowances to buy tickets to the live personal appearance of a big band or a singer that was appearing at The Palace Theater.

As we look at the downtown as it is today, it's hard to visualize how it was in the past. From 8:00 in the morning till almost 4:00 the next, it teemed with life and exciting things to do. So you see, this is why I developed a love affair with the city. And this is why, even to this day, I do not see it as it is, but as it was. It will never return to its glory days, but so long as there are those who can remember, memories live on.

Laura A. Byrnes

GLENWOOD AVENUE

Racing the storm.
Your lightning eyes
Finding the north star,
Our laughter drifting, mingling,
Singing with the crickets.

The shivery evening breeze
French kisses
The back of my neck.

Love me
Like a convertible ride
On a hot summer night,
Free, head-on, eagerly
Vulnerable for this joy.

Patricia Olson

EAST SIDE

    The East Side of Youngstown was the place of my birth in 1938. If only people who live there now could have seen it then, it was beautiful and safe. Not only weren't there drugs, shootings, or other crime, but the doors didn't even get locked -- day or night. We moved from there when I was only seven years old, but I have memories locked in my mind.
    We lived within walking distance of the Wilson Theater. What a place! Different movies three times a week. Not only one feature film, but two, plus cartoons, and a special feature which was usually the current news of the county. Wednesday night!! That was the time to go to the **show**. Free dishes too, and they were Carnival Glass, now considered collectibles, although somewhere along the line they got tossed out or broken. What I'd give for a set of those dishes now.

We loved to go to the candy counter, where for five cents you could get a big Hershey bar or any other candy that you wanted. Maybe it's just a childhood memory, but those five cent Hershey bars seemed twice as thick and three times as big as the ones that now cost $1.50. Further down Wilson Avenue at the corner of Center Street was an outside market, and a free (or almost free) clinic where our doctor was Doctor Schwebel, who was from the Schwebel bakery Family. We were at the clinic at least once a month and at the market every week.

Another favorite store on Wilson avenue was Zidian's Market. Fresh meats and cheese and always a sample when you went in to shop. The market is now LaRussa's Italian products, and the family is also Zidian Realty. They're from my heritage, Lebanese, although they whip up great Italian products.

I remember my mother giving me ten cents to go down to Zidian's and get a loaf of bread. It was an uphill walk from the store to my house, and being a kid, I carried the loaf of bread under my arm. In those days it was wrapped in a sort of waxed paper package and was sealed at each end. I must have been holding it too tightly, because when I got home, there was only half a loaf. The slices marked a trail from my house to the store. I really cried, because that was ten whole cents wasted, and Mom didn't think that "half a loaf was better than none."

Then there was the great new food invention -- oleomargarine. We'd fight over who got to press the orange dot in the middle of the white soft package and squeeze it until it turned to bright yellow and was supposed to taste like butter. We thought it was great, but I wouldn't eat it now on a bet.

We used to spend a lot of time playing in Lincoln

Park. In fact, I can remember quite a licking because I walked down there without telling anyone where I was going. We lived on Ayers Street. I didn't think it was such a big deal. My Dad always told us that he put the crack in Council Rock and we believed him.

I hate to use the phrase "those were the good old days," but somehow they were. We were in World War II and I can remember putting blinds down and shutting out all the lights whenever there was an air raid. I can remember Mom feeding the hoboes when they came to the door. I remember the man delivering coal and shoveling it down the coal chute. The potatoes baked on the ledge of the coal furnace door were crisp and delicious. I can remember the ice man and the horse pulling his wagon. The knife and scissors sharpener would walk down the streets calling out his trade in sing-song and we'd beg Mom for something to sharpen.

The times were harder though. Mom scrubbed the floor and waxed it every week and then we had to cover it with newspapers so it would stay clean until Sunday. Double Dexter washers, clotheslines for drying. No such thing as permanent press, so ironing was on Tuesday. The phone was a party-line, and you had to know which ring was yours or you'd be answering someone else's call.

There was the Ritz Bar on Wilson Avenue. I was only six, I but would hear my aunts and uncles talking about the fun they'd have going there to dance.

Wilson Avenue was just one of my memories, and even though there weren't many conveniences and the war was going on, it was safe. Neighbors cared. No crime or maliciousness. Our doors were always open. And everyone was as happy as I was.

Madelyn T. Sell

JUST THE TWO OF US

Unlike today, most mothers didn't work outside the home during the forties and fifties; they were able to spend more time shopping with their daughters.

During the 1950s in Youngstown, a typical mother-daughter outing consisted of a trip downtown via the city bus. There were no malls or plazas, so shopping downtown was a major event. We embarked upon the shopping trip by boarding a bus on the corner of Shehy and Truesdale Streets. Wearing our mother-daughter look-alike dresses made the trip even more special. My mother was truly spending quality time with her six year old in 1952.

There would be shopping at most of the grand stores like *McKelvey's, Strouss, Lerner's, Baker's,* and my favorite, *Livingston's*. In those days, a girl with a Livingston's dress was definitely chic, even at six.

Shopping wasn't the only adventure. This was an all-day trip which had to include a movie and lunch. A movie at the Palace was the highlight of the day. If we got to sit in the balcony, it was even more exciting, for I could hang over the railing on the second floor. Looking down from the railing, I could see all the people. A magnificent crystal chandelier hung from the ceiling and extended through the center of the circular railing. What an elegant sight!

After the movie the decision had to be made on where to eat. There were so many fine eating establishments in Youngstown during these years. Would it be *Rodney Ann's, Strouss' Grill, Hollander's, The Italian Restaurant.* Whichever one we chose, I knew we definitely would have a chocolate malt at the bar in Strouss' basement and take home a coconut cream pie from Strouss' bakery counter or a strawberry whipped cream cake from the *Federal Bakery* next to Livingston's.

Mom and I still shop together. We still spend quality time. But nothing comes close to those memories of trips by bus to downtown Youngstown.

Dorothy Jones Honey

A TWENTY'S HOLIDAY PLAN

Family picnic at Idora Park, 1920s

Picnic day at Idora Park was ecstasy in living color. When Aunt Bertie and Mother got their heads together to plan our big summer treat, all six of us kids could scarcely contain ourselves until the special day arrived. The weeks of anticipation played themselves out in imagined ups-and-downs on the roller coaster and jerky, dizzy whirls on the whip.

The capricious weatherman loomed as the potential villain in our scenario. For the entire week before *THE DAY*, we studied weather forecasts, searched the skies each morning as if to forestall any collecting of dark, ominous storm clouds and peppered heaven's gates with whispered prayers for blue skies.

We knew time was running out when Mother rescued the picnic basket from its winter hideout and began filling it with all sorts of goodies. Carefully positioned first in the basket, Aunt Gwen's specialty, a three-layered yellow cake, had chopped nuts and cherries nestled between layers and sprinkled abundantly over the iced top and sides. A goodly wedge of this always climaxed the picnic menu. All of us, eating our way through tasty, moist potato salad, ham sandwiches, Boston baked beans, crisp pickles and stuffed olives, saved room for Aunt Gwen's cake.

Our time schedule on *THE DAY* had to be split-second accurate, for the two families met on the Diamond, arriving there on different bus lines, to board the Park and Falls car. With bated breath we watched town-bound passengers disperse on the southwest side of the Diamond; we heard the clanging conductor's bell wildly signaling Federal Street of the car's intention to swing around to the southeast side of the Diamond for South Side and Park-bound passengers. To be at the head of this line of waiting streetcar riders, a must, we could make our dash the minute the doors opened. Looking neither right nor left, we bee-lined for the rear of the long streetcar; there the seats contoured the rounded end of the trolley. We could all sit together in a semi-circle with by now two heavily laden picnic baskets and other carriers fitting neatly under the seat.

Everyone relaxed a bit as the car moved on its steel tracks up Market Street, cut over Warren Avenue, out Glenwood, on to Parkview and then came to its final breathtaking rounding of the bend into the park itself. With the cool greenness of Mill Creek Park at our backs, shrieked warnings in our ears about not leaving anything behind, we hopped off the streetcar to behold the majestic dance pavilion with its intricately carved decor and the joys and delights of Idora Park spread before us. Paradise at last!

Juanita Hall

WILDCAT

When it burned down
Victim of a welder's torch
It was ranked
The seventh best coaster in the country;
The best of the wood rides.

The rattled climb,
Like pulling a rusty chain
The shakey turn.
You always sat on the wrong side
And got squooshed.
The descent and the screams,
Like all the cats in the world
Seeing the approach of a tidal wave.

I rode when I was young
Beside my father
Who always reached
His arms into the air
As I hung on and begged him
To do the same.

The tickets were 5 cents apiece,
Six for a quarter,
Or twenty-five for a dollar.
It always took 5 tickets.

I rode with boys
I enjoyed being squooshed
While pretending that I didn't.
I rode with my sons,
Who were braver than I
Except that Timmy hated the screaming.

The coaster burned down
And the park died.
The merry-go-round and the silver plains
Were sold and taken away.
The Jack-Rabbit still stands
Near the desserted ballroom.
The plan to use the dance hall
As a Christian hotel fell through,
Lack of financing.

Weeds have grown in both parking lots
But you still can see The Wildcat
From the road.
Trees hide the scars of the fire.
The ride looks whole
Except there are no screams.

Mark Reed

GHOST WILDCATS

1.
Over vast eons of time
glacial rivers of ice flowed,
what would be Youngstown
lay buried underneath
10,000 years ago
creeks started carving through glacial till
sculpturing the Mill Creek Gorge
in what was just a tick in the clock of time,
Iroquois and Delaware Indians
traveled through these ravines
on their way to the salt licks at Mineral Ridge;
as a boy,
my tennis soled feet traveled these same moccasined trails,
a ten year old pretend Indian on the warrior's path
through all of this,
the creek
cascading
churning
splashing
flowing
falling
rumbling
reverberating along the rock walls;
just recently,
added to this calliope of sounds
was the tumultuous wooden rumble-thunder
of the coasters above,
at Idora Park.

2.

Clickety-clack
clickety-clack
clickety-clack,
chains going,
pulled tight on meshed gears
drawing skyward an open gondola car of nervous humanity,
sweating hands clenched tightly on padded bars,
feet pressed firmly on the metal floor deck,
a few brave souls reach skyward in mock defiance
of impending doom,
the wooden skeleton hill sighs and strains,
timbers bow
creak
pull tightly back
and all holds true;
the car crests,
arcing over the top,
chains and gears ease their tension,
let go,
as the gravity engine takes over;
now the hearts race
and the screaming starts,
poised on the edge of the abyss
and each and every one of the passengers
realizes the folly of tempting fate
because if the car jumps the track . . .
but it's too late now,
there's no turning back
back . . .
back in time receding into memories
the thunder cars rumbling
only in the soft gray matter which comprises our brain
quiet returns to the gorge
the gurgling creek its only voice now
But I remember
I was there

Lucy Hite Murphy
Diane T. Murphy

MEMORIES OF IDORA PARK

My fondest memories are of *Three Cent Day* held each summer. It was for the children during the Depression. The years I remember most are 1933-35, my teen years.

We would ride down Mahoning Avenue to town on the streetcar. There was a pass in the paper that let you ride for nothing. We changed to the Idora Park streetcar downtown. Those cars were very special because they had velour seats, not leather.

We went swimming at the pool first. While our hair dried we rode rides and had french fries or ice cream cones. Then to the penny arcade across from the roller coaster and merry-go-round. The boat ride in the Tunnel of Love was great fun. It had lots of scary things lit up as we went by, heading for the ride down the hill where we were sure to get sprayed.

In the afternoon there was dancing at the Dance Hall. I don't recall that it cost anything. The band was always good and we danced with other friends who went from other schools.

At three o'clock I had to start for home before my friends did. My dad worked seven to three and supper was on the table promptly after he got home. He worked five days a week, one hour on then one hour off. Actually a four-hour day. But everyone got the same. The hour they didn't work the men played 500. He got to be a pretty good player.

I headed for the exit near the merry-go-round. It exited down to the Silver Bridge. I hiked along Lake Cohasset almost to Pioneer Pavilion, up over the hill to Old Furnace Road. There were no homes in that area then, except a family by the name of Lipps that lived on the corner near the drive to lower Bear's Den. I went up and over what is now Rocky Ridge and waved to my mother, who was waiting in the kitchen door of our home on McCollum Road at South Hazelwood.

Ruth Merolillo

LIFE IN THE TWENTIES

Driving along the freeway one day, between the East Side of Youngstown and Boardman, Ohio, I sadly reflect back to the past, to the home where I was born, and the streets I played on that are no longer in existence because of this freeway. If ever there was a time one might call the *Good Old Days*, it was the twenties, before the crash and the onset of Depression.

My memories of the twenties include: playing in the streets until it was dark or walking along the sidewalk without fear. Doors could be left open on warm nights without fear of being robbed. Numerous walks along South Avenue with my older cousin to see Charlie Chaplin at the movies Downtown because automobiles were scarce during these years. Most of us walked towards our destination, often several miles.

Children were never bored; we played wonderful games: jump rope, tag, hide and seek, bouncy ball, jacks, marbles, and building our own kites and flying them! Often I was reminded that we were like the *Our Gang* kids. Life was happy and easy from ages four to seven. Relatives lived close by for love and comfort. But the onset of the **Depression** changed things.

I could see my father pacing the floor, holding his head between his hands, muttering and groaning despairingly. He'd been laid off from his job at Sheet and Tube and his concern was how he would be able to buy food and pay the house mortgage. After a few weeks money ran out and he, along with many others, took a pot down to where soup was being served. Those who lost their homes went to live in shanties made out of large wooden crates. It was named Hoover City because so many were living under these conditions. Many were blaming President Hoover for the Depression. Having discussed matters with Mother and relatives, my father decided to sell his home and locate a farm that was affordable.

Soon afterwards, all going according to his plans, we moved to a farm he had purchased. The farm was overgrown with grass and thorn bushes, throughout the sixty acres. Obviously it hadn't been lived in for a very long time. The house was run down and needed fixing. Sadly, I realized that there would be no friends to play with and no relatives to go to. Father bought a cow, two horses, chickens, and some farm equipment.

For a while, we lived on milk and eggs. Mother made butter out of cream and baked bread on a coal and wood stove. We had no electricity, furnace, bathroom, or refrigeration. We bathed in a wooden barrel using water that was heated in a large kettle on a coal and wood stove. Kerosene lamps were used at night. Also, the outhouse was our toilet facility. Winters were cold and on a windy night snow sifted in through the window frames. Bricks were heated, wrapped in towels, and taken to bed. Mother had a large goose feathered tick, I used it for a bed covering.

My father's men friends and relatives would stay for several weeks at the farm to clear the land of the grass and thorn bushes with a sickle. They would cut down trees to make posts for barbed wire fencing to hold the animals in the pasture. Mother shared the work load and was often tired from her chores.

As time went by the farm gradually came to produce enough to sell or donate. The Depression had been a struggle for many, but the values I learned were those that remained with me throughout my life, the values of appreciation, patience, and love.

Dorothy Jones Honey

WW I
(As Told Me by My Mother)

The battle's done.
The war is won.

Headlines scream;
Newsboys shriek;
The fervor reaches
A tremendous peak.

The children marched from Roosevelt School
With teachers leading, two by two,
High aloft in each chubby hand
Waved a tiny flag; both, pride of our land.

WW II
(As Lived by Me)

The Fuhrer's beat,
At last, defeat.

I boarded the bus with hopes on high
To get to New York to meet that guy.

The trip to town was A-OK
Through town, Himrod to the B&O
Was not for any faint-hearted Joe.

People had massed wall-to-wall
To celebrate the victory call.
I left the bus with suitcase'n all
And pressed and pushed through that human wall.

To board that train on time for me
Was the goal of my flight through the human sea.
I made it! And soon was New York bound
Where one war weary gent waited for me.

Nancy Bizzarri

THERE SHE IS

There she is
in the ubiquitous long
raincoat and sexless
junior league bob,
banging on the
front door of
the St. Vincent DePaul.

Ignoring the city
birds up on the
wire, who chirp,
"Side door, Side Door!"

But to get
to the side door,
she must walk
under a wire
over a muddy path
through downtown
revitalization's idea
of a flower bed.

Or all the way
around the sidewalk
into the parking lot
where the poor people
park Japanese cars
with temporary plates.

These things she
will not consider.

So she stands,
determined,
at the front door
banging,
heard by no one.

For it is said:
That it is easier
for a camel
to go through
the eye of a needle
than for a rich
woman to get in
the front door
of St. Vincent DePaul.

Rosemarie Policy

SHE REMEMBERS

In her heart, clock has never turned.
Changes of modern times,
Her spirit has not learned.

She sees the days long gone by;
I can see them too
When I gaze into her eyes.

Crowds of people line the city streets.
Downtown Youngstown is the place to be.
Five and dime is where they meet.

Dressed up from head to toes,
She is a sight to see.
Her skin a radiant light, her lips a budding rose.

The people celebrate,
Laughing and waving to strangers as they pass.
They all seem to have such promising fate.

She sits down on a bench to rest for a while
And looks at the place she calls home.
The women walk with grace and style.

She remembers good times as she speaks of the past;
She smiles like the young girl that she was.
She is faraway and dreamy and leaving fast.

That beautiful lady looks up at my face,
Takes my hand in hers.
Tells me stories of the greatest place.

Little shops and restaurants, the theater and the banks--
All the places she used to go see.
For her freedom, she gives thanks.

She can never go back-- it wouldn't be the same.
People do things differently now.
She is running out of time in her lifelong game.

As long as there are photos and grandchildren to tell--
She will spin her tales of Youngstown,
A place she loves well.

Paula J. Mckinney

THE SNOWMAN

I watched *Frosty the Snowman*, a trite and asinine Christmas special, last night. I like the song, love the book, hate the TV version. It insults a child's intelligence. As usual, the TV people killed it.

Waxing nostalgic, I remember well my first snowman, December 1941. People in readers were always constructing snowmen . . . beautifully molded, white, constructed personages with hat . . . pipe . . . scarf!

Well, with this idyllic vision in our heads, my girlfriend and I proceeded to construct (she knew how). "We just make a ball and start rolling it till it's big," she said. The snow had been there one day already so it was all black and crummy. We rolled and rolled around my friend's back yard in the winter dusk. Round and round in the coal and sulfur air.

The snowman grew and gathered up large deposits of cinders, old dead leaves, little sticks, some bone pieces, a shoe heel, and narrowly missed some dog unpleasantries (we were observant).

Finally, the size was right for the body. "Now we start the Top." Oh well, round and round again. By now the yard was minus quite a bit of snow and it looked pretty bad. Now for the final touch -- a hat! Eyes! Pipe and scarf! We found some rocks for eyes, nose and mouth. Coal was a necessity of life. No parent in a state of right mind would let us adorn a snowman with it.

What for a scarf? Well, we each had one but being of sound six year old mind, we had enough brains to hang onto it. An old hat? Well, having no father, I had no man's hat. My partner's father in this venture had a hat, but the general opinion was that he'd prefer to hang onto it so we chucked that idea. A pipe? Her father smoked cigarettes and due to the war they were very scarce. Even the butts were cherished till they were mere nubs. "How about your father's pipe?" she said. Oh my God! No!

Pop's pipe reposed on the mantle under his picture, was dusted with care and considered on a somewhat sacred scale. Ma would skin me! By now we were cold, wet up to the wrists, and it was almost dark, and . . . oh well.

She went in and I plodded up through the back lot and up the sixteen back steps into our kitchen. My coat was a mess. My mother was mad as it had to dry out to wear to school in the morning. "Hang it in the cellar way and put your mittens on the oven. I should think you'd have better sense."

The befouled Vesuvius stood till its fortunate demise due to the thaw. I don't think most people knew what it was or cared. Things just didn't work out like in the readers. No jolly neighbor complimented us on it. One or two may have glanced and said "What the hell?" God knows it didn't come to life. Just as well. There were enough human wrecks in the neighborhood already.

Keith Barkett

*Glacier Drive
Mill Creek Park*

Patricia W. Cummins

FANNIE, MY FRIEND

It was the day before the birth of my second baby when Fannie came to our house. Heavy with the unborn child, I had been unable to bend over to clean in hard-to-reach places. It was embarrassing to show dust and crumbs, but that was the reason I needed her. My next door neighbor had a very nice helper who came every week. Playing outside with my young son, I had come to know her and I had asked her if she had time to help me, too. She replied that she didn't have extra time, but that she had a neighborhood friend who might be interested. The result was Fannie, my friend for more than forty years.

From that first day, we were compatible. Never a student of domesticity, neither caring nor qualifying, Fannie became my teacher. Everything I know about the care of furniture, washing windows, arranging cupboards and closets, scrubbing floors, and politics on Youngstown's East Side was learned at her side. My babies were her babies, and she still called them that long after they were grown men and women.

When we met, Fannie was thirty-seven years old and I was twenty-six. She had come with her husband, Willie, to Youngstown from Tennessee ten years before when many black people came to work in the steel mills. Their home on Verona Avenue, off Albert Street, was neat as a pin. Willie, who worked in the Open Hearth Department at the Ohio Works of U.S. Steel, kept the hedges along the front walk clipped to perfection. Treats from their flower and vegetable gardens were shared with us. Fannie was the personification of the Christian woman. She sang in her Greater Friendship Baptist Church choir, served on the mission committee, and visited the sick.

Fannie and Willie never had a child of their own, but they raised a God-child named Corinthia. That little girl was from a troubled home where the mother suffered from a mental illness that, at times, was life-threatening to her children. Fannie and Willie took the child into their home and raised her with the love and care she needed. So, besides homemaking, Fannie and I shared parenting. That included not only the fun times, but also heartbreaking times. Fannie had a wonderful sense of humor . . . and a wonderful sense of caring. Once, putting my older son down for his nap, she said she must wash his face because he had Oreo cookie around his mouth. He replied, "Fannie, you have Oreo all over you!" She thought that was hilarious, and repeated the story for many years. After their God-daughter had lived with Fannie and Willie for some years, her natural mother took her back again. Fannie was worried, and rightly so. Finally, through a social services agency, it was discovered that there were no utilities in the house, and that the mother was building fires in the kitchen to heat food. Authorities discovered evidence of fires on the table and on the floor. The little girl returned to live with Fannie and Willie.

The lunches we shared featured foods our families wouldn't touch. At the top of the list were black bean and bacon soup and split pea with ham soup, sometimes out of the can and sometimes out of Fannie's pot. Her favorite sweet was saltwater taffy although her teeth were terrible and in her older years there weren't many of them. She loved fruitcake, and our annual gift cake from our second cousin twice removed always found its way to her table.

She was a very intelligent woman who had broad interests including community issues and worldwide concerns. She read the daily newspaper and often took magazines home from our house to read. Together we heard the news of Kennedy's assassination. Fannie cried because she feared it might be racially motivated. I had heard tales of her train trips South to visit relatives, and how at certain depots she had to change cars to sit in the **Coloreds Only** coaches. My own children were growing up knowing the love and friendship of a black woman, and none of them felt prejudice toward people of color.

She helped move us twice. We were in such *sync* that she could pack and unpack cupboards and bookshelves, and we both knew where everything was! The second move was out-of-town and our friendship depended on the mail. All of us looked forward to her letters. When she was joking or teasing, she would write **smile** at the end of the sentence so that we wouldn't miss the humor.

In her teen years, Corinthia's father moved her to Detroit, which was another traumatic wrench for her God-parents. After working at U.S. Steel for more than thirty years, Willie was the victim of an infection that attacked his heart and made him an invalid. Corinthia heard of Willie's illness and came back from Detroit to help Fannie nurse him. One of Youngstown's most notable surgeons told me how much respect he had for Willie. He said that when he came to office appointments, he was dressed in his best suit as if he were going to church, a real gentleman.

After Willie's death, Corinthia continued to live with Fannie. She was nineteen and became pregnant. The young father was still married to someone else. Fannie then assumed the responsibility of grandmother. She taught the daughter she loved as her own that "There is more to life than being a welfare mother," a direct quote from Fannie. She adored the little baby boy, nicknamed Tank. During Willie's illness, she had devoted herself to his care, but after his death she came back to help me, and, in addition, she began taking care of my husband's offices. Corinthia had gone to work, so on some days, Fannie took Tank with her to the office. He became very fond of my husband; we really had a whole family friendship.

There were weddings in our family, and there was a wedding in Fannie's family. She supervised a beautiful wedding for Corinthia in the chapel of Friendly Bells, taking care of every detail-- a true mother-of-the-bride. Soon there was another little grandson for Fannie to dote on. We were becoming grandparents on a regular basis, and Fannie became acquainted with the babies of our babies. She kept photographs of them all in her living room. Our nest was empty, and as we were working full-time, our visiting time was less, although our friendship was just as strong.

The baby nicknamed Tank, now a teenager, often stayed with his Nanny to keep her company. She worried about his safety on Youngstown's East Side with the drive-by shootings and drug traffic. Under her influence, he was growing into a fine young man who became a member of a junior Police Corps. You could feel his love and devotion to this elderly woman. Now we were both older, widowed, and retired, and for some years Fannie's knees, asthma, and sinus condition had been slowing her down. Inevitably, the tearful call came from Corinthia, beloved Nanny had died.

Fannie had left Greater Friendship Baptist Church because it was too difficult for her to get there. She had joined the small church around the corner on Willow Street, Morning Star Missionary Baptist Church, and that is where her funeral was held. Four ministers were there to eloquently celebrate her life. Her two teenaged grandsons took part; Keith, always referred to as the Baby, played a trumpet solo, *How Am I Supposed to Live Without You*, and young Larry (Tank) read a wonderful poem which had been written by Fannie. Selections by the Senior Choir were memorable. Corinthia stood up in front of the Congregation and sang Fannie's favorite, *His Eye Is on the Sparrow*, in a voice that would rival Aretha Franklin's. She sang music that filled the church and our hearts. She sang Fannie into Heaven. An elderly gentleman pianist closed the service with *I'll Fly Away*, and I left with the love of Fannie, my friend.

Diana Shaheen

SARAH

    She smiled benignly at him, picked up her needle, threaded it with a green yarn and began her autumn project, a muted green and gold woven comforter with a cobalt blue eagle at its center. It was the featured project from the September 1979 issue of *Needlecraft*. The coffee table had the netting for the cover placed carefully upon it, waiting for the designer's touch. Sarah sat on one end of the couch while John sat on the other end, cutting the yarn for her into equal lengths. The room was small; it contained only a couch, two chairs, and a coffee table. The natural lighting was poor. It would have been better except for the tree that covered half of the small bay window that let in only morning light. It was compensated for by a large brass floor lamp that stood to the right of Sarah. The two overstuffed arm chairs sat empty in the early evening's shadows by the window. The house in which Sarah lived was a renovated old mansion on the North Side. It was divided into six medium-sized apartments. Sarah's apartment was on the ground floor. The advantage to this was that she had the use of the front porch. The disadvantage was that the North Side was not as safe as it had once been, and a ground floor apartment left its occupant vulnerable to vandalism and theft. Sarah, like many Bohemians in the area, was drawn to this side of town. The hospital where she worked was close by, as was the University with myriad attractions, as were many of her friends.

John was staring at the faded cushion on the tripod footstool, a colorful needlepoint of the old schoolhouse with the classic bell in the belfry, and the block figures for students. It was an example of Sarah's great-great Russian Grandmother, Bubba Bolinki's, handiwork. Sarah began to weave the green yarn in and out of the netting as John casually placed his feet on Bubba Bolinki's masterpiece.

Sarah could remember as far back as ten years old, sometimes further, and with every memory of any craft she had ever pursued was Grandma Bubba Bolinki's footstool and John. The presence of John, and Bubba Bolinki, as the tripod became familiarly known, always meant open shop. John and Sarah had grown up together on the West Side as the boy and girl next door. As dissimilar as John and Sarah's heritages were, they could easily be mistaken for brother and sister. Both had high cheekbones, ruddy complexions, and red hair, and both their families believed strongly in the work ethic. John's father had worked the assembly line at GM, and his mother had worked as a secretary for the Cafaro Company. They had invested well all of their lives. Between the two of them, they had succeeded in sending their two sons through college. Though all of their children had grown, they still maintained the family home in town and had purchased a winter home in Florida. John could trace his roots to the Mayflower on his mother's side and to the Cheyenne on his father's side.

In contrast, Sarah's roots were Eastern European and Mediterranean, Russian on her mother's side and Italian on her father's. Both her mother and father were second generation. Sarah's father's father had a grocery business on the East Side which he passed on to his son. After World War II, the business boomed, and in the 1950s, Sarah's family and the business moved from the East Side to the North Side where Sarah was born. While the business stayed on the North Side, she and her family moved to the West Side. Here they settled, becoming close friends with John's family.

John and Sarah were odd companions. Wherever Sarah went, around the block, or halfway around the world, all she had to do was to begin a craft project, any craft project, knitting crocheting, woodworking, jewelry making, sewing, whatever, and John would appear as if by magic. If she wanted to pursue any craft, it seemed she had to accept the presence of John and his sanction or objection as he placed his feet firmly upon Bubba Bolinki.

More than once, Sarah had conveniently taken the Bubba to a junk yard and quietly left town, hoping to lose dear John in the process. Amazingly, the moment she began her seasonal project, a knock was heard at the door, any door she was behind, and in walked John carrying Bubba Bolinki. He would suggest in his most motherly tone that Sarah should be more careful with her family heirlooms, and that it was most fortunate that he knew where to find her, for someone had callously discarded Bubba into a junk heap in the last town they were in. But what were friends for and why didn't she tell him she was leaving? Sarah mumbled an "unknown" under her breath, swearing she had left word with his landlord who said he was out of town on vacation and wouldn't be back for two weeks. ". . . And by the way John, you owe me one hundred twenty bucks for your overdue rent . . ." It wasn't her fault that his landlord didn't give him the message, but if he didn't give him the message, how did he find out where she was anyway, "huh, John?" And John would swear he only had her best interest at heart and he found out from her mother where she was, who also had her best interest at heart. It was very foolish to leave town without telling anyone; besides, what's a brother for? She would pat him on the head, smile benignly, and reiterate that she was free, white, over twenty-one, and he WAS NOT her brother! Besides, she was quite capable of taking care of herself, and who invited him anyway?! She was an R.N. with a specialty in ICU and could move anywhere in the country and find employment. However, after five years of moving from one town to another, she decided to get in touch with her roots, which were, as far as she was concerned, in that part of town in which she existed before her connections with John. She wondered if his being a computer analyst and programmer had anything to do with his uncanny ability to find her. After these minor blow-ups, a long pause ensued. Sarah would sit back waiting for a response she knew would come and John would sit there highly amused at what he would term "another one of Sarah's impotent tirades."

"Well, now that that little tirade is over with, let's see what you've got here?" At this point, he would give his oblique critique on her latest project: "This color's too bold . . ." or "Isn't that the wrong kind of yarn to use?" Why did she have to get a different-shaped needle for this, as far as he was concerned the type of needle she used on the last project would have worked just as well . . . . He would go on and on until Sarah would let him assist her in some picayune way, like holding the clew or cutting the yarn or watching the kiln, anything to shut him up.

Whatever she did, he had to help or she wasn't allowed to work in peace. Usually, when John arrived, other friends would drift in, one after the other. The last couple of times, however, it had only been the two of them. It seemed as though their group was getting smaller and smaller as one by one they married or settled into a profession or had children and lost contact with one another.

Sarah watched John as he methodically cut one strip after another; she imagined that the yarn was jute and John, in a noble gesture of acceptance of his plight as her unrequited lover, agreed to meet her demands and willingly offered to hang himself for lack of her love. Self-immolation at the foot of her divine altar-- ah love . . . ah fantasy . . . .

"Ah Shit! John! You're not cutting them long enough!"

"That's seventy inches, isn't it?" he said. She measured it.

"That's sixty-five inches and you know it! You pig! You goddamn shit-head!" He had never been so careless before. Usually, he was too precise.

"Give me that footstool!" She proceeded to yank the tripod from under his feet, and in a rage of fury, posited Bubba Bolinki soundly on John's inglorious crown. Their eyes met, both stunned. Sarah calmly picked up the fallen tripod, and examined it. She took one more look at John's shocked facade. Hopefully, he would see her differently, not as his sister or the girl next door or anyone he had a connection with, but as someone separate from himself.

"You can go home now John, my precious heirloom is still intact and I don't need you around to mess up my craft." She placed Bubba Bolinki on the couch beside her; he reached for the tripod, trying to reclaim it as his own for having been its rescuer, but in anticipation of just this act, she immediately rose and clutched it to her person.

"No, no John; Bubba Bolinki is my heritage, not yours, after all, I'm the one who's of Russian descent. My grandmother made this tripod, not yours. Yours came over on the Mayflower, remember? I'm the immigrant's daughter and you're the All-American Son! So get out and leave this goddamn foreigner alone!" He swiftly moved toward the door, still stunned by her not-so-important-tirade. "The next time you think of dropping in, do us both a favor and phone first." His eyes quickly scanned the apartment for the location of the telephone. He did not see one. She, guessing what he was thinking, gave him her best Cheshire Cat grin. He slammed the door after himself.

Alone, alone at last! Sarah stood staring at the closed door. In a flash of indignation, she rushed to the door, locked it, bolted it, and put her back against it as if the mere force of her willing it could stop John from ever entering her apartment uninvited again. Hot tears of rage slowly began to trickle down her cheeks. He had no right to follow her the way he did. He had no right to walk in whenever he wanted. How did he know when she was going to start a new project? Who told him? Did he follow her around to the different shops when she was purchasing supplies? How did he know to the exact hour when she would begin each project? What gave her away? What would happen if she refused to let him in anymore, what then? She searched her memory for a similar situation.

Carol had a friend like John except that they had been lovers and had lived together for three years. When she broke off the relationship, it took years for him to stop calling on her. Finally, for safety's sake, she and Jesse moved in together. Jesse had had problems similar to Carol's, only worse. Her ex was a junkie with a habit a mile long. He expected her to feed, shelter, and clothe him as well as support his lifestyle. When she refused and left him, he followed her from her home to work and back again. Sometimes he broke into her house and stole any extra cash she had around. Finally, she got a restraining order. But John was nothing like that. He was just overbearing, insensitive, and obnoxious. He would never hurt her. He just had to know where she was all the time.

Sarah wiped her eyes with the back of her hands and slowly, deliberately, went into her bedroom, locked the door, took the phone from under her bed and plugged it into the jack on the wall. She tried Carol and Jesse's number, but the line was busy. It was just as well. She was too upset to talk rationally. She began to remember other women who were followed by ex-lovers, or well-intentioned male friends, or brothers, or fathers, or sons. There was always some male following some female for something she was supposed to provide, whether it was comfort, solace, protection, sex, love, contacts, connections, other women. It seemed there were expectations that men had of women that had to be met on cue or there were consequences. Suddenly Sarah was fearful that she was missing her cues and she was unaware of what the consequences might be.

She unplugged the phone and shoved it back under her bed, got up from the floor, and frantically began to check her record collection for something soothing. She reached for an album of Bach's fugues, set the album on the turntable, set the needle on the Fugue in G-Major, hooked up the speakers, unplugged the sewing machine, and plugged in the stereo. Slowly, almost methodically, the vibrations in the room began to change from stifling sobs of futility to heaving shudders of anguish. The music crescendoed, and the calm of despair's flurry reinstated itself.

Gradually, the music began to penetrate, lifting her into another dimension, soothing her, and she thought about other women enticing her, absorbing her, bringing back memories of past emotions that had foretold future happenings. The more closely she listened, the more clearly she heard whispers of a not-too-distant past. The voices of broken promises and forgotten dreams both exhilarated and saddened her. When the air cleared, all that was left was the silence of obscure future. She wondered about the different voices in the fugue: "What would it be like to be part of a fugue, a single voice in an ensemble of players?"

Lilly M. Green

PEACH BLOSSOMS & GALVANIZED STEEL

Walter Street no longer exists. The huge, brown, wood-frame house that was home to me, my parents, my grandmother, my great-aunt, my brother, and my two sisters for many years is now pleasant memory.

Yes, Youngstown has undergone drastic changes over the past forty years. Although some might dwell on the negatives, this community has influenced my ideas, my values, and my worldview in positive ways. My earliest dreams and ambitions were formed on the lower South Side in that special house that was a unique combination of today and an era long past.

Home and family ties were important when I was growing up. My mother was a fantastic homemaker. Everything was always immaculate, polished, or neatly ironed and starched. Our floors were so shiny and clean they could have been used in television commercials. Yet adults and children alike felt relaxed and comfortable when they dropped in to visit.

Our house sat at the top of an enormous hill just perfect for sledding in winter and rolling down in the summer. An old-fashioned grape arbor and a vegetable garden took up most of the back yard, and peach trees intermingled with apple trees to form a border on the right side of the property.

At the young age of seven, I placed little importance on certain material things I consider a necessity today. I loved the neighborhood and the neighbors, and there was always something interesting to do and someone to do it with.

Because of the closeness of my family and our neighbors, we kids had an abundance of positive reinforcement and numerous adult role models. My father worked at U.S. Steel; but with eight people to provide for, money and possessions were scarce at times. But the love, caring, and sharing of relatives and friends more than made up for material things we lacked.

My fondest memories of that house center around the screened-in side porch. There we socialized, played, entertained, and enjoyed many pleasurable activities. It was also the place where my mother took out the big round tub many nights and gave all of us kids our baths. Oh, our house had indoor plumbing and toilet facilities (in the basement), but it didn't have a bathroom. Our friends who did have real bathtubs envied us and often begged to spend the night just so they could bathe in our shiny, galvanized-steel tub.

The year I turned ten, the city purchased and demolished all of the houses on Walter Street, Hilker Street, and several other surrounding streets to extend Route 680. Only the Pepsi Cola plant that was across the street from my house survived. My family and I moved into a beautiful two-story house further up on the South Side. I loved the new house and spent many happy years there, but I will never forget the innocence and purity of childhood on Walter Street.

Josephine E. Minor

BAG LADY
Charcoal

Khepri C. Polite

CAT OWNER

    I sit on the couch in my house on Elm Street and look into the shining eyes that are looking into mine. They seem to look with such intensity, such purpose . . . searching mine for something. Not finding it, they casually look away and peer into the dark recesses beneath the couch. I notice the slight expanding of the pupil, the heightened tenseness of his stance. He springs . . . at what I can only guess. What the hell is that cat springing at? And what does this cat want from me? For that matter, what have all the cats throughout my life wanted from me and why?

    Cat Owner. These two words seem most often applied to a human who feeds, shelters, and cleans for one or more cats. However, what do the two words *cat owner* really imply? I'm personally more inclined to this definition. Cat Owner: A cat who owns something. Used in a sentence: The cat owner's human loves to feed, shelter, and clean up shit for his master.

I do all these things for my cats. Plus, open doors for them to go outside . . . to go inside. I build houses, nests, caverns, ledges out of boxes, and lay open brown paper bags around the rooms. I let them sharpen their claws on me, gnaw on me. I'm endlessly concocting new amusements for them. I let them sleep on my head for Christ's sake. I feel guilty moving them from a chair. They lounge on pillows while I lay out lines of catnip for their pleasure. I sing to them, do dances for them. When I'm not funny or entertaining to watch, they give me the cold shoulder. I'm left in the middle of the living room, in my underwear, standing in a brown paper bag singing Crosby, Stills, & Nash: *Chestnut brown canary, ruby-throated sparrow*, and they wonder just what the hell I'm doing. How dare they walk away from me! Who do they think they are with that smug, self-satisfied look on their faces? Then they have the nerve, after walking away from me, to spring into the corner after . . . NOTHING! I yell at them hurt, "What do you see in that empty, bare corner that you don't see in me?! I should be getting your praise . . . ME!" I slink to my room and close the door, sulking. Once again, an outcast in my own home. I hear them padding softly, triumphantly, outside my door.

I watch, with a slightly crazed look in my eye, as a black and white paw is shoved beneath my door, into my room, clawing . . . at Nothing. Damn you! Leave me alone! The paw withdraws.

Shortly, I hear what sounds like a plastic garbage bag being ripped open. Ha! Now I have you. I run out of my room with a rolled-up paper to exact my revenge. "I told you . . . ." Not a cat in sight. Damn! Where? I go back to my room. I sit down and rub my eyes. I get the feeling that someone is watching me. I open my eyes and there, across the room, staring at me, sits one of the cat owners. She speaks to me. "Meow?" "What?" "Meow?" "What!" She stares. I glance over at the paper bag in the middle of the room. I sidle over to it, and turn it on its side with the opening facing her. I say, "Meow?" She looks at me, looks at the bag, walks over, smells it, and goes inside. Ha! I grab the bag and close it. Laughing to myself, I then open it. She walks out looking demeaned, but poised. I say, giggling, "Guess I let the cat out of the bag. HeeHee." She looks at me probing, seeking . . . not finding what she's looking for. Once again   . . . I have failed. I don't care anymore. I grab the squirt gun and give her a couple shots in the ass, knowing that I'll probably fail even more miserably next time.

I yell at them, "You're aliens. I know you're aliens. You can trust me with your secret. I am worthy. I won't say anything . . . . why did so many ancient cultures revere you! Why!" As I blubber this, a cat owner jumps effortlessly to the arm of my chair, crawls into my lap, and purring contentedly, goes to sleep with a knowing smile on her face.

Frances Duffy Taylor

THREE HICCUPS and a BARK

It was moving time again and I was excited because at last I had found a house in beautiful Mill Creek Park, Youngstown's answer to stress reduction. Moreso than the house, it was the location which enchanted me, although the house, too, was what I wanted, a lovely four-bedroom ranch nestled in the trees on a secluded tiny cul-de-sac with only four other houses. My house sat in the middle of the lot of them with no other houses behind it or in front of it. The backyard view was that of tall pine trees extending the horizon and the front view was the treescape of the park. It was mandatory to offer a grateful "thank you" to Mr. Volney Rogers, the benefactor of this beauty, for his vision. Without any street noises or commercial activity nearby, it was "graveyard" quiet. As a matter of fact, it was almost too quiet, so I thought about a dog as a noise factor. The two of us could romp and explore the beauty of nature together as we travelled along the lakes and fishpond and ran across the various bridges, like the Silver Bridge, from one scenic view to the other. It would be fun and we would eat well and sleep well and dream of our next adventure.

Dreamily, I sat on the steps and closed my eyes and was immediately transported to Fellows Riverside Gardens. Looking at the beautiful flowers and feeling the spray from the flowing water fountain mist my face, I watched a wedding taking place at the gazebo and the bride and groom having their picture taken at the end of the garden where you could see the river flow. Then, I remembered that to be married by water symbolized "good luck." As my eyes followed the manicured lawn to the matching weeping birch trees at the other end of the garden, I saw the trees nod their leaves to the movement of the wind in a beckoning motion to come and enter the newly established flower and vegetable garden to see the experiment taking place there. But, before I went there, I decided to walk by the lovely arches and lattice work dividing the roses and highlighting the perfectly arranged beddings of annuals in full, colorful bloom on the other side. Stopping to read the stone plaque sitting amidst the purple verbenas I sighed when I read "In memory of my wife -- and mother -- Joseph R. Vasey." But it was the concluding sentiment which touched me the most. It read, "For the enjoyment of those who pass this way." How kind, how generous, I thought. This is what the "milk of human kindness" must mean. So I silently thanked Mr. Vasey for his. Arousing me from my reverie, I heard a dog bark and construed the intrusion as an affirmation that I should get one too.

Yes! I said to the air, I will get a dog.

Blessedly, I didn't have to look for a dog. I just threw the thought out into the universe that I wanted one and lo and behold, a young neighbor saw me in the yard one day and stopped to tell me about his misery. His story was that he had been given a puppy by a friend and his mother wouldn't let him keep it. "Will you please take him so that he won't have to be sent to the pound."

"I will be delighted to take him," I told him, and went out and bought $145.00 worth of dog supplies in anticipation of the new arrival.

He was just a twelve week old, brownish, male puppy when I got the little fuzzball. Part shepherd and rottweiler with the most unusual markings of four amber colored stripes on each side of his upper chest made him look like a little tiger when he sat upon his hind legs. Very, very cute, he was. *D. John, IV*, I named him. It was the name of the other three dogs my sons had had and since I couldn't think of any good reason to contrive another, I used it again. Docile and gentle, but a whiner, from room to room he would follow me around as if I were a dog-mother. But, as he grew, his teething and chewing on everything became my bane. His instincts, too, were so defined and wildish that it was difficult for me to discipline him. Well, I wanted a dog and this was all a part of the package, so I was told.

One morning I awakened unusually hungry and cooked a man-size breakfast of bacon, eggs, fried apples, toast, and coffee. The aroma filled the air and wafted throughout the house on the morning breeze blowing into the kitchen window and made me feel even hungrier. I was just about to sit down to eat when the phone rang. Running to the living room to answer it, I thought, I'd find out who it is and call them back. While it took only a few minutes to answer the phone, it was still too long. When I returned I stared in disbelief at the near empty plate. Only the toast was left. "*D. John!*" I screamed into the contented-looking face. "How could you!" Then, I laughed. The delicious-smelling aroma was too irresistible, even for a dog.

I should have named him "Slick" because *D. John* became very playful and clever very quickly. His favorite trick was waiting until I was in bed and lying very quietly. Then, he would come to the side of the bed and sit, look at me, and whine. When I wouldn't move and he was convinced that I was sleeping, Zoom! He would race into the den and jump upon the couch. Wham! He would hit the floor, then leap into the chair. Zoom! He would race into the kitchen and rattle his food dish and drink water. Then, back into the bedroom he would come, jumping on his bed to gnaw his toy bone and chew on his dried pig ears. Back and forth he would go, running and jumping and whining until he was exhausted. Never once did he bark, just whine. Somewhere along the line I would fall asleep to the tune of his antics. In the morning, however, he would be sleeping as if he were a little angel. Oh! how cute I thought, until one night he chewed the buttons off of my antique couch and got himself corralled to the basement, until . . . .

I was so anxious for our romps and to see him retrieve my thrown sticks. I fed him the best puppy food and vitamins. As a result, he grew quite large. As he grew, the seasons changed. Before I knew, winter was melting into spring and the warmth of the sunshine was irresistible. To better enjoy the rays I opened the kitchen door wide and sat on the first step of the three steps leading to the outside. *D. John* was sitting on the landing right behind me when I heard him hiccup the first time and turned around to look. As I watched, he hiccuped a second time and stared at me, puzzled, as if I had done it. Right after those hiccups, which seemed equally spaced, he hiccuped a third time. Lo and behold then, to the surprise of both of us, he let out the loudest bark I've ever heard. The sound of the bark scared him; he looked funny; I laughed and hugged him, soothing his alarm.

This was a momentous occasion because my darling little whining puppy had just become a barking dog and I was one of the few fortunates to witness this dog experience. With another hug, I congratulated *D. John* on his new "doghood" status and cooked him some bacon as a gift for his barking maturity.

He was now ready to romp the park, to bark, and so was I.

*Silver Bridge
Mill Creek Park*

Keith Barkett

Randy J. Abel

TSUNAMI

When the Old Man comes to visit, we have lunch at *The Beat*-- soup, foccacia, coffee. Dad loves the "beat blend" and serves it to his buddies back home at their poker gatherings. He takes pride in explaining that it's the special concoction from a coffee house where his son works in Youngstown, Ohio. I figure they couldn't care less where it comes from, only that it keeps their old asses awake long enough to ante next hand. But Dad goes on and on about his son, who wants to be a professor of English or Literature or Some Shit. "Here's a picture, and something he wrote about the family; here's an old letter he sent from the Middle East, terrified: 'watching death fade into the horizon . . .' helluva line there." Dad's pride seems to know no boundaries. Mine runs in different currents.

Back at *The Beat* I introduce Dad to the gang and imagine each of my friends and acquaintances to be instantly overcome with powerful new understanding of who I am and from what sort of stock I spring. As if I'd coached him beforehand, upon meeting two professors, Dad refers to himself as a "displaced steelworker." I'm grateful for his choice of phrasing.

See me now in the light of my glorious birthright-- Son of Displaced Steelworker! Displaced to the second power, Proletarian Pugilist cast into the Post-Industrial suck-void. Buffed surfer on the bitchin' curls at the leading edge of the rolling tide of accumulating despair and nothingness. Know me now, my compatriots, to be a Steely Sanctified Warrior among you!

At the counter, Dad makes his usual eighty or ninety corn-ball wise-cracks, then apologizes to an amused Jen for his "silly banterings."

"Oh my God," Jen laughs, "I thought Randy was the only person on earth who used that word on a regular basis. Wow, Randy, this *is* your father!"

And there's certainly no denying that . . . however, there always seems to lurk some shadow of the old shame-- lingering remnants. "To be the very blood of that hated blood," as Charles Bukowski said, "made the windows intolerable/ and the sounds and the flowers/ and the trees ugly." These were times when Wayne's "silly banterings" were made vastly less entertaining by the constant presence of booze on his breath and a bar stool on his ass. Sometimes there was venom in his words that pushed me to Mom's side of their constant battle for our favor. "*Whatsizname*," she would call him, or the more impersonal "*Whatizface*," which I understood to be the most powerful obliteration of Dad's humanity.

What's his face? I must have wondered. His face is that round, stubbly, strangely scarred thing that banters, snores like a chain saw, eats ham hocks and peanuts, sucks down Pabsts like a flabby Popeye without spinach, bristles my cheek as sandpaper when we hug and floats in my dreams like a sing-along ball-- always away, away: through the GATX plant to his girlfriend's apartments through the Glass Tower Lounge and off into the darkness, away, away where it pops with a loony-toon **pfwt** *like a bubble in the head of a frost mug of draft.* **Pfwt**.

But now there's a pride in owning our kinship,

and a safety in everyone's having known me first--
their having gotten the facts sifted through in my own
style, my convenient packaging. My banterings have
prepared most of them for this meeting, and Dad
provides living proof of my blue-collar genes, which I
choose to cling to at the moment as my gritty reality.

After lunch we take a drive along the Mahoning to
look at where all the old mills were. I play Tom Waits
tunes, hoping to increase the Urban/Industrial feel of
the afternoon. Dad is put-off by the discordant parts
and would probably rather hear a "light rock" station,
though he doesn't say so. I imagine that the Old Man
and I will at some point get out and stomp around on
old slag piles, kicking scraps of metal, maybe finding a
battered lunch box or clipboard, but I'm the only one
dressed for it (me in my steel-toed flight deck boots,
Pops in his Keds) and Dad's kidneys are making even
car sitting an arduous task. There's still much to be
said and felt and I have big expectations for our
next-day visit to the labor museum.

My older brother, Greg, is with us at two o'clock
the next afternoon, when we head to the museum after
coffee at *The Beat*. We three are the only people in the
place as Dad wanders, giving rapid commentary to
almost everything he sees. Pointing to the round
fountain-sink in the locker room display he tells us: "I
was working once in a part of a foundry that didn't
have showers . . . and I got so dirty that I had to put a
brick on that foot-control thing there and climb into
this damn thing . . . my whole body in a fetal position.
Worked, though. Damn you got filthy in that soot!"

But he doesn't linger on the eyes in the photos
like I expect him to, like I find myself doing. When we
get to the one of the worker with half of his calf
sheared off, Dad says, "Look at his face . . . they must

have him drugged so far out of it that he doesn't give a shit about anything." My take on the guy's look was vastly different: I saw a placidness in his eyes, an intense strength, a mark of struggle-- but now I'm not sure. A model of his old mill catches Dad's attention and I'm reminded of a familiar pillar of our family's labor connection-- the Old Man's passion for expounding the minute details of every one of his toiling endeavors. From hot-rolling to dish-washing, the finite motions of the mundane were a mainstay of Wayne Abel's bar stool and lounge-chair litanies. I feel like I could have written the Standard Operating Procedure manuals for all of my father's nine hundred occupations . . . like I could have walked in cold and performed tasks with the ease of an old-timer. Maybe that's why I ran screaming from Dad's bars to my school books: there had to be jobs out there that just couldn't be interpreted in a four-hour sitting.

When my time to work draws near, we all leave the museum and Dad and Greg head to Struthers to visit one of Dad's old mill buddies. On the porch at *The Beat* I give my father a hug and our faces are sandpaper and sandpaper. He is Dad in sweat pants and Keds and kidney problems and no pension. I am his son in Y-town-- displaced, dysfunctioned, dicking-around on the flood plain.

I return to the Ocean, where the Tsunami still roars and rages toward the infinite void. It has finally peaked. I am shooting the curl -- terrified, naked. Tsunami, tsunami! Teskete, teskete!

Somebody yells "Now!" and I step into the abyss just as I hear another voice scream, *"TSUNAMI!"* and the world becomes soundless, boundless motion . . . Except for the rush, somewhere in the turbulent silence, of a running tap-- and farther off, the sound of a Hank Jr. tune on an old juke.

It was the summer of 1988. The old man had just kicked my ass all over a pool table for the third time, and we were in the head of the Mechanicsburg VFW pissing-out Yuengling, a cheap Eastern Pa. beer with octagonal beehive bubbles composing its head-- like an alcoholic mosaic or rip rap.

Out in the bar waited an assortment of Dad's buddies that must have been time-warped and transplanted from the Glass Tower back home. Like the Tower drunks, the Mech'burg vets offered shooting tips and regarded me as a protege-- an upstart young buck who wasn't quite yet in on the game but was already thirsting for it, bellying up to it. And it was apparently Dad's intention that night to make the *primary rule* more clear-- to pass it on to me just as it was accorded him. Present it like a treasured heirloom he could place in the palm of my hand.

I have loved some women

Bocephus was emoting and I noticed with a measure of drunken disdain that the old man wasn't washing his hands.

And I have loved Jim Beam. . .

"Kid, I want you to know something."

But they both tried to kill me

"Yeah, Pops." I was about to turn off the faucet when he grabbed me by arm, turned me to face him.

Back in nineteen seventy-three.

"Listen, I don't love you and I never did." His eyes were cold, vacant. He seemed to be angelically white-- looming and hovering.

Over and over,

"You needed to know that."

I wonder how I go in this condition. . .

The tap was running. "Whatever, Dad . . . the tap

is running."

Somewhere in the abyss, the Old Man and I are shooting stick in an old, beat pool hall-- straight out of *The Hustler*. He's wearing Keds and sweats, I'm in my flight deck boots, jeans, and Harley-Davidson t-shirt. We both drink Squirt from funky green bottles. As I rack 'em, Dad reaches back under his shirt to scratch the area of a pimple on his right shoulder. It must be a hurter; he scrunches his face-- his eyes squinted intently with the exquisite pain, and I notice that they look just like they do when his attentive listening explodes into laughter, those uncontrollable peals that rock his whole form, but store their focus and intensity in the deep, fatty recesses of that squinting.

When did I learn to mine those depths, seeking to glean transmissions of acceptance and joy? When did I first laugh into a mirror and know that laughter is not a billion ripples of joyous surprise, but the squinting twinkle of my father's eyes?

I've racked the balls tightly by a method taught to me by the old man long ago-- alternating solid and striped, with the eight-ball in the center, buffered. Dad takes a swig of Squirt, chalks his worn old cue, leans, squints, takes his aim and thrusts-- clean-blasting a dead-on solid sledgehammer-- shockwaves of clatter, chaos, conception.

"O-kay!" he laughs. "Christ, Pops!" I cry.

Dad has sunk the seven, now he's dropped the two, now the three. I'm afraid that he'll run the table, but as he takes aim on the four, he miscues and the ball skips off and onto the hardwood floor with a thunk and a roll past two other tables, finally stopping as it meets the bottom of the men's room door. We both laugh as I retrieve it and gauge my first shot-- eleven in the far corner pocket; I miss completely.

I swig my Squirt as Dad misses another shot. Then I hit the eleven into the side, but on the next shot bank the fourteen off the rail and right up to the left corner pocket, where it kisses Dad's three and rests there like a kinetic conspiracy. Pops and I both shake our heads, grinning; then he chalks, bends to it again and proceeds to run the table like a two-bit, punk-ass hustler (which he was and is). I'm disgruntled and pride-struck as he saves that damn three for last-- taking several angles of approach before executing a shot that kisses my fourteen into his three, and both of them into the pocket.

"That's the way it goes m'boy . . . the best-laid plans . . . *c'est la vie, c'est la vie*. All right, Randolphski, show us your stuff." And into the large end of his cue like Keith Jackson, "It's been a rocky start for Abel-the-Younger thus far, folks, but I'm sure we can expect *big* things from the Young Buck here on out!"

And I hit the twelve, then the nine, then ten, thirteen, fifteen. Dad is brimming as I check my angles on the eight aiming for the corner by which he stands. Behind him, the proprietor watches, sipping Schlitz; behind him I can see typhoon rains outside the pane glass, in the red-blue neon glow of the Void.

"I say, keep your eye on the ball, Son. Eye . . . ball. Eyeball . . . that's a joke, Son, cain't *eat* it!" Dad's Foghorn Leghorn is awful, woefully unsouthern, but it does its job of breaking my concentration with a laughing moan. I chalk to regain composure and take my aim again.

"Remember, Son . . ." Dad starts suddenly. I glance at Dad, at the proprietor, at the Void.

"It's all about English."

Smiling, I thrust and sink the eight **solid**.

My break.

Madelyn T. Sell

72 and STILL STEPPIN'

Jerry was a great dancer. He danced with many great bands. Oh how he had rhythm! Fifty years ago, he and his sister, Rita, were a team in the Youngstown area. He remembers as if it was yesterday. Now as he waits on the aerobics floor of the gym, he is hoping the bright, energetic instructor will opt for some *swing music* to do her routine by, instead of *that wild '90s music,* as he calls it.

Five minutes to ten, Jerry positions himself in front of the instructor's platform. He is wearing his Bally's sweatband, of course!

"What you gonna play today?" he shouts.

"I got a new tape of some 90s songs," the tall, attractive instructor replies.

As the instructor begins, Jerry is eagerly ready to step. He looks around and begins to follow the instructor's directives and the beat of the music.

"Hey, I'll give anything a try," he shouts. Everyone laughs, but they admire the drive and love of music this seventy-two year old Navy veteran has.

As I watched Jerry in the mirrors which surrounded the floor, I noticed he gave a little swing before he stepped up onto his step. It was if he wanted o break loose and dance one of those swing dances with his sister, Rita, just like they used to do some fifty years ago. He seemed to be yearning for the Big Band sounds. The sounds of the Dorsey era. He and his sister danced with the Dorsey band in the 40's when the band came to Youngstown.

"That's enough for me," Jerry shouted. It is only halfway through the class and he stepped out for a few minutes. But he came back and gave it another shot. Never quitting! He kept plugging away at all the new steps the instructor threw at us.

"Pfew! That was wild!" he said. Everyone was starting to walk off the floor to put away their steps. I waited for my daughter, the aerobics instructor, as she gathered her gear. Jerry hung around, too.

"Hey, I like you," he shouted to my daughter, "but where's that other girl who plays the big band sounds when she teaches?" he inquired.

"She teaches the nine o'clock class," she replied laughingly.

"Is she your sister?" he turned to me and asked.

"What a compliment!" I thought to myself.

"No, I'm her mother!" I hesitantly said. We stood there and laughed together.

"Where ya from?" he asked.

"I'm originally from the East Side of Youngstown."

"I used to live on the East Side, too." His eyes lit up and instantly it was as if we had a common bond.

"Hey, wait here," he said eagerly.

Before I had a chance to say anything, he hurried toward the men's locker room. What could he be doing, I wondered. Nevertheless, I stuck around, since my daughter wasn't quite ready to leave.

He produced a worn wallet from which he pulled out a snapshot of a handsome couple. It appeared to be taken professionally.

"This here is me and my sister, Rita," he boasted. "This picture was in front of the Idora ballroom and the Nu-Elms dance hall when we was performing with the Tommy Dorsey Orchestra."

His eyes swelled with tears as he held the frayed photo. He recalled so many years and continued with his stories of starring on the same bill with Cab Calloway and Paul Winchell in the '50s. Though the ten o'clock aerobics class had long been over, we stayed to hear more of Jerry's stories of music in Youngstown. Those days have come and gone, but Jerry is still steppin' to the beat!

Sylvia Centofanti Stefani

80

Born March 9, 1916, in the beautiful town of Introdacqua, Italy, I've reached a great milestone in my life: eighty years of age! Flashes of the past flood my mind. So many memories!

My dad had been coming back and forth to America (Youngstown, Ohio) since he was a teenager. After I was born, my dad, Luigi Centofanti, returned to Youngstown to work at General Fireproofing, saving money to bring us to the United States.

When I was four years old he sent for us: my mother Adelia, my brothers Frank and Sal, and me. We took a slow, packed boat to Ellis Island, were placed in quarantine, and then were finally processed out. We took a train to Youngstown. Dad met us and took us to our home, which he had ready, at 451 South Pearl Street, and which had a large garden. The neighbors were fantastic. All different nationalities, but we were all *family.* We arrived in April, 1920.

Ours was a dead end street with a rolling meadow below and a road next to the railroad tracks. Every evening the neighbors would gather with jugs and bottles to get water.

In 1929, my dad and I were in our garden when a large, dark man running up from the tracks cut through and said to us, "Don't move and don't chase me!" We were so surprised we just stood there. In a split second, he ran through the back adjoining garden onto South Garland Avenue. We heard a shot and ran to see what happened. We found our neighbor Mr. Mike Antonucci had been shot and killed. It was so tragic, so senseless. If we had moved or whatever, it would have been my dad and I. I've never forgotten it!

Up on our corner of Wilson Avenue, we had the Wilson Theater, an A&P store, a doctor's office, and a streetcar we could ride for seven cents downtown to Central Square. Everyone went to the Wilson, especially on *dish night, bank night,* or any other time something free was given. We all had sets of dishes.

Going to school was a great experience for us immigrants. I started in kindergarten at Shehy School. On the last day of school, my teacher, Mrs. Begin, took us all to Lincoln Park for a picnic and told us about Council Rock and the Indians and all about the park. Later, I went to Lincoln for Junior High then to East High for four years, graduating in 1933 in a class of 133. We had a wonderful time. Money was scarce; unemployment was rampant. We were in the midst of America's worst Depression and a banking crisis, but we were graduating! *Good* dresses (silk, chiffon, georgette, etc.) cost $3.00. Cotton dresses were $1.00, but were worn as house dresses only, not for *dress-up*. Evening gowns averaged $5.00 to $6.00. We did not wear caps and gowns, which would have been a waste of money we didn't have. A $2.00 pair of white leather pumps sufficed for all the services and the banquet. A fifty-cent pair of silk stockings and new undies came to a total of about $20.00 for most of us, plus the cost of the banquet. *We had it made!* My gown cost the royal sum of $6.00. It was a beautiful shade of sky blue in a georgette cut on the bias (old-fashioned terminology), which made it hug the body. It flounced out at the bottom from the knees to the ankles. It had capelet sleeves and a V-neckline. As I was leaving I picked a pink rose from our bush and pinned it on my dress. I felt like a queen! Our banquet was for classmates only. It was the highlight of the week and was held at the Youngstown Country Club (Yes, we had a band). We carpooled and many a father taxied his sons and daughters and their friends. We did not have limousines, corsages, or outsiders for dates. No makeovers, tuxedos, designer dresses, all-night parties, and other expensive frills like today's graduates. We danced, talked, intermingled, and enjoyed our last night together. Now, sixty-three years later, what goes around comes around. Looking at today's clothes, I saw a dress that was called a *new look*. It was body-hugging and flared out at the bottom from the knees to the ankles. It had *new styled* capelet sleeves and a V-neckline. It was almost a duplicate of my 1933 gown. Our gold graduation rings cost $6.00. That is no misprint. We were all poor! It's a good thing we never knew it. We were happy and contented with our lot.

    During the Depression we would have picnics at Mill Creek Park, Idora Park, and Lincoln Park. Idora would have three-cent days; movies were a dime. We would walk to the Isaly's for five-cent cones. We did a lot of visiting and walking around the block.

When Mother wanted to treat me, she would say, "Let's go downtown and get a California." Oh Boy. Served at the counter of McCrory's, it was a hamburger with a slice of tomato and french fries. It was special because no one went out to eat. We didn't have money to spare. We walked to town and did a little shopping then rode home on the streetcar. Later, the bus came and took over.

On August 25, 1920, women were given the right to vote, and the feminist movement had its start. The *Roaring Twenties* was known as the *Flapper Era*. Short skirts above the knees, rouge, and lipstick. It was shocking. (My, how times have changed!) We had prosperity for eight years. October 29, 1929 brought the Great Depression. The worst year was 1932. Many lost everything they owned and jumped out of windows to their death. In the 1930s, a Ford car was $550, a three-bedroom home was about $5,000, and gas was twenty cents a gallon. Everyone thought prices were too high because money was scarce. When Dad received $3.00 a day in wages, we thought we had it made. Soup kitchens became a familiar sight in Youngstown. Many needy people were begging, *Brother, can you spare a dime?* After Pearl Harbor was attacked on December 7, 1941, war was declared. On May 14, 1942, we lined up for ration books. Sugar, butter, coffee, flour, etc. were rationed. Tuesdays and Fridays were meatless days. Men's suits were sans vests and their pants had no cuffs. At home, we did our part with the popular slogan, *Use It Up, Wear It Out, Make It Do, Or Do Without*. Manpower was so scarce that my friends and I became *Rosie the Riveter's* until the summer of 1945 when our boss told us to get our tool boxes because we were through. The war was over-- Thank God!

In 1946 we purchased the historic Kelly's Hotel with two other friends at Ripley, New York. Whenever I was asked where I was from, I would say we had a business in Ripley, but we were from **Youngstown**.

In 1962 we sold the business and returned home to Youngstown. We built in Austintown but to me it's still Youngstown proper. Too bad all the suburbs were not incorporated with Youngstown. Joining Silver Leaf Garden Club in 1964 opened new doors for me. We were all very active in the Garden Forum of Greater Youngstown. I started exhibiting in Forum flower shows and at the Canfield Fair. Many of us went to Judging School. I became a nationally accredited Master Flower Show Judge, which takes a minimum of thirteen years to acquire. I also was appointed Consulting Rosarian by the American Rose Society and received their Bronze Medal. I was a member of Ikebana International No. 70, which studies the art of Japanese arranging. Most of our garden clubs have asked me for programs and classes on arranging and horticultural know-how. I've been very glad to oblige.

My husband Vincent and I were talking about slowing down. He's a hunter, fisherman, mushroom and dandelion picker, gardener, etcetera, but life would be so drab without our beautiful flowers to look at. A few years ago I joined the *How to Write Your Own Life Story* class at the Multipurpose Senior Center in Youngstown. So here I am typing this at midnight because it's due tomorrow. Slowing down-- I wonder!

Dorothy Jones Honey

THE WAY IT WAS
(At Youngstown's East End)

    Vivid yellow, like the winter sun, pyramids its shaky self into the night. An orange wanting to be red forms a pulsating border for the yellow; it in turn is fringed by a burnt rust cloud, the entire patch of brilliance losing itself in thousands of fiery specks.

    On the ground stand shadowy buildings. A great dark blot seems the immediate source of the gold-hued splash against the tinted southern sky. Weaving in and out this man-made rainbow roll waves of rusted dust. Alternately seen and unseen beyond scorched clouds loom regularly lined stacks. Out of the top of each disappears a thin, now white, now grey, now black, veil.

    To the north the dark night sky stretches lazily over the earth, heedless of the excitement in its neighboring air dome. I look back to the spectacle of color and admire man's creation.

Juanita Hall

SCRAPBOOK

I have photographs somewhere
Of the trip we made
To Canada when I was eight.
One of me and my sister
Posed in front of a tee-pee
I was dressed in a striped shirt
That made me look even fatter
Than I was at the time.
And pedal-pushers,
The style of the fifties.
They were pearl gray.

I have souvenirs of that trip.
Toronto in '58.
A small canoe and a bark tee-pee,
Salt & Pepper shakers
With *Thousand Islands, Canada*
Written on them in gold.

I have memories
Of that family trip
To the Falls.
One of my mother
Slipping a huge black
Rubber rain coat
Over a sheer lilac summer dress.
The coats and boots,
Squishing and squeaking
As we walked
Underneath the Falls.
Big hats hiding our eyes,
Covering our hair.
We rode on the *Maid of the Mist.*
I later bought a comic book
About her legend.

I have pictures,
Ceramic images,
Legends of my own.
That trip we took
Long ago,
One summer.
Our family
Preserved in the photographs.

Paula J. Mckinney

HOME AGAIN, APRIL 1963

The gentle evening air smelled of freshness, smelled of the forthcoming Spring. A touch of sulfur and coal smoke mingled with the promise of new green. The last sheet was off the line, smelling of the steel mill at the end of the street.

Just last night, the kids had a big fight among themselves over "Does the wash smell like the mill, or does the mill smell like the wash?" As usual she had to play peacemaker between the two sides. Actually, everybody was right. Five kids could sure cause a fine fuss when the humor was on them.

The lights were on in the house and it was time to start the bedtime routine. Wednesday night . . . bath night for the girls.

Nevertheless, she stood a minute in the long narrow backyard, with its greening grass and the nice little patch at the end of the yard, between the hedge and the garage, where she intended to put in a garden if the landlord didn't object.

She took several good deep breaths of the fine smell of the mill, basking in the feeling of stability it had brought her since childhood. So good to be back!

Youngstown felt grand!

She straightened her back, firm as the steel that ran in her veins, mingled with the blood of hearty *greenhorns*, walked into the house.

Francie Magnuson Kerpsack

STEELMAN

He had a dream, not so big a dream,
But perhaps the biggest dream of all.
He would be a part of it,
An honest part of it,
And do his job best that he could do.

He did his job for 40 some years.

Then one day his eyes lost their sparkle.
And doing the job didn't seem so important.
He was not part of the dream anymore.
It didn't matter that he was the best around,
That he had kept his side of the bargain.

It didn't matter anymore.
He had been betrayed.

The company sold out! Sold out!
The men who had invested their sweat and good
Labor were as nothing, as nothing.
It happens all the time, all the time.

And now there is no one who understands,
There is no one who sees the big dream.
If you disregard the least of these,
My brothers, you have disregarded the dream.

I pity you who never understood the bargain.
I pity you who have cursed our young
Men as you threw away their fathers,
As you compromised the dream.

Suzanne Kane

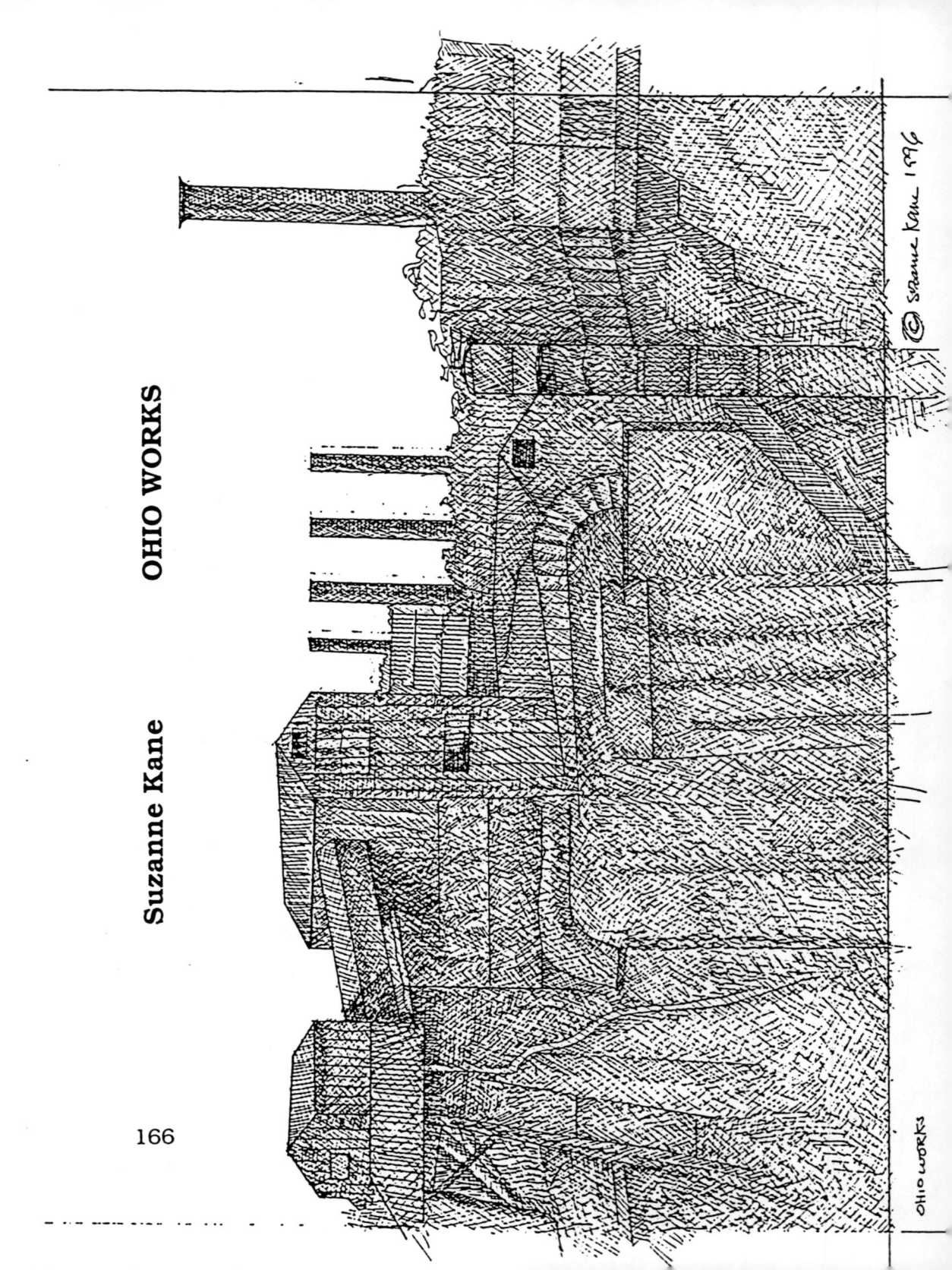

OHIO WORKS

Edward G. Manning

MAHONING COAL RAILROAD COMPANY

Youngstown can boast of having had one of the most profitable railroads in the world. It was the *Mahoning Coal Railroad Company*, incorporated on February 25, 1871. The line was formed when coal mining was the Youngstown area's main industry. The railroad company was organized to haul coal from Trumbull County to the iron mills in Youngstown. The heavy density of coal and iron ore traffic over the line's right-of-way accounted for its ample profit. In fact, it was one of the most profitable railroads in the world.

The transport system in the Mahoning Valley from the early days contributed a vital role in the industrial development of this area. The first roads were Indian trails that were laid out on the migrations of the buffalo in prehistoric times (Wilcox 88). Later, turnpikes, canals, and railroads were constructed. In the first part of the nineteenth century railroads were locally owned, and extended less than a hundred miles. Now, one local railroad was unique; it was the Mahoning Coal Railroad Company, which was incorporated on February 25, 1871 and capitalized at $70,000, and then growing to become one of the most profitable lines in the world. It was organized by William Bonnell, Augustus B. Cornell, David Himrod, and Joseph and Richard B. Brown (Corporation Records 70). Earlier, in 1826, coal was discovered on Mary Caldwell's farm in the Crab Creek area (Butler 769).

The Crab Creek section encompasses the northeastern section of Youngstown. Her farm was in the vicinity of the present Thornton, Saranac, Logan and Kensington Avenues. Definitely, the owners of the Mahoning Coal Railroad Company were entrepreneurs.

Earlier, in 1846, the Brown brothers with William Bonnell founded the Youngstown Iron Works. They named it the Brown-Bonnell Company in 1854. In 1899 it went into receivership and out-of-town capitalists bought it and named it the Republic Iron and Steel Company (Butler 182.) Previously, Augustus B. Cornell was granted a franchise by the Village of Youngstown (June 15, 1865) to erect a gas plant to supply gas to the residents of the Village (Youngstown City Ordinances). The gas works was located at 317 East Wood Street. Also, Cornell was in partnership with David Himrod in the operation of the Himrod Furnace Company, which was located on the present site of the William B. Pollock Company on Andrews Avenue. Incidentally, they had to remove a mound to make way for the furnace.

Unfortunately, Youngstown was landlocked when coal was discovered. After the discovery of coal Youngstown changed from a farm community to a coal-producing area. The coal was the best in Ohio, high in carbon and free of sulfur and impurities (Comley 37). The coal sold at a premium price. Its trade name was "Brier Hill." Then attorney David Tod, who served as Postmaster at Warren during the administration of President Andrew Jackson, used his political influence and business acumen to get a canal for Youngstown.

Finally, with federal grants, state aid, and private capital, the Pennsylvania-Ohio Canal was in operation by 1840. Now, the first canal in Ohio ran from Cleveland south to Portsmouth on the Ohio River.

This canal joined the Pennsylvania-Ohio Canal at Akron. It flowed east to Kent and Ravenna, then turned southeast to Newton Falls, Warren, Youngstown, Lowellville, and on to Beaver, Pennsylvania, where it joined the Ohio River.

Certainly, the cross-cut canal opened up the markets in the East and South for coal, wool, and dairy products. Then, in order to promote the sale of coal, David Tod went to Cleveland and asked the captains of the lake steamers to try coal in their boilers. Much to their satisfaction they found coal to be more efficient than wood (Butler 769). A ton of coal gives more heat than the same amount of wood, and takes up less space. The canals carried most of the freight until the 1850s (Morrison 478). Then the railroads replaced the canals just as the canals supplanted the stagecoaches and wagon trains.

Furthermore, the trains ran all year, whereas the canals were frozen in the winter. Here in Youngstown there was a network of rail lines to the various coal mines to haul coal to the main lines. The Mahoning Coal Railroad ran along Crab Creek on the north side just east of Youngstown State University. The line ran to Brookfield, Andover, Struthers, and Sharon, Pennsylvania. The total trackage was 92 miles.

Now, what made the Mahoning Coal Railroad one of the most profitable in the world was its right-of-way. There was heavy coal traffic from the mines of West Virginia and Pennsylvania to the docks at Ashtabula for shipment to the Northwest. Likewise, the iron ore from the Mesabi Range in Minnesota and Lake Superior Region was loaded on lake steamers and shipped to Ashtabula, where it was loaded on hopper cars and hauled to the mills in Youngstown, Pittsburgh, and Wheeling. Although the Mahoning Coal Railroad owned no engines or cars, they were paid for every car that went over their right-of-way. Earlier, clerks kept record of the number of cars going over those tracks; later, computers counted the cars.

Undoubtedly, the earnings of the Mahoning Coal Railroad were an investor's dream. It earned $2,307,834.00 in 1966, which was its best year (*Moody's Transport Manual* 726). The stock reached a high of $725.00 a share. Its earnings for a train mile exceeded $25,000.00 The road was capitalized at $15,000,000.00. The line could have been called the Mahoning Gold Railroad. Its annual dividend averaged $35.00 per share.

Ownership of the line was not as fixed as its rails. In 1884, the local owners leased the road to the Lake Shore and Michigan Railway Company. In 1914, the New York Central bought the lease and held it until the New York Central merged with the Pennsylvania Railroad in 1968, forming the Penn-Central. Locally, John Tod, Vice-President of the Youngstown Sheet and Tube Company and a philanthropist, was a director of the Mahoning Coal Railroad Company (*Youngstown Vindicator* 20). Finally, on February 18, 1982, 111 years to the week after its incorporation, the once fabulous railroad was liquidated, paying its stockholders $16.5 million, or $550.00 a share. About 83 percent of the stock was owned by Penn-Central RR.

Definitely, Augustus B. Cornell, one of the original owners, was a civic and industrial leader. He served on the Village Council and was treasurer of the Youngstown Hospital Association. Incidentally, his residence was at 624 Elm Street on the present site of Youngstown State University. Richard Brown's widow donated money for a chapel at Elm and Woodbine, and known as Richard Brown Memorial Methodist Church.

In summation, in the early part of the nineteenth century, "canal fever" spread across the United States and a network of canals were constructed to transport coal, farm products, and manufactured goods. Then railroads replaced the canals because the railroads were faster and could operate all year. It was also cheaper to build and maintain a mile of track than a mile of canal. But railroads, having a monopoly, then raised freight rates and passenger fares. This rekindled "canal fever" a second time in a century. However, by this time the railroads were too powerful, economically and politically, and they thwarted the efforts of the canal promoters.

Surely, the Mahoning Coal Railroad was an exception with its excessive earnings. But as the steel mills reduced production, so was the need for coal and iron ore diminished. Also, the iron ore in the Mesabi Range is almost depleted. Now, the iron ore is coming in from Africa, Canada, and South America. The once fabulous railroad is no more. In this valley the iron, steel, manufacturing, and railroad industry has come full circle from its humble beginnings in 1839 to its disastrous demise in the 1980s.

Works Cited

Mahoning County Recorder's Office. *Corporation Records*. Vol. 2.
Butler, Joseph G. *History of the Youngstown and
    Mahoning Valley*. New York: 1921.
Comley, W. J. *Ohio: Future of a Great State*. Cleveland: 1870.
Moody's Transportation Manual. New York: 1966.
Morrison, Samuel Eliot. *Oxford History of the
    American People*. New York: 1962.
Wilcox, Frank and William McGill. *Ohio Canals*.
    Kent, Ohio: Kent State University Press, 1969.
Youngstown Vindicator. July 16, 1936.
City Council. City Ordinances. Youngstown, Ohio: 1907.

172

173

Marguerite Wilbarger

EXTINCTION

Have you seen the blackened lairs
Down along the river
When the stir of life in there
Set the earth aquiver?

Then at dawn their heaving breath
Billowing and steaming
Pillowed us in cottonwood
Smug complacent dreaming.

Did you see them-- fierce and bright
Glaring eyes of fire
Staring from the cave of night
Then the flames leaped higher?

Streams of workers then would pass
Through the massive door
Serve a monstrous repast
Tons of coal and ore.

When I sing of blackened lair
Crumbling to ruin
When I tell of dragons there
Where are those who knew one?

We have watched the magic go
Roofs of lairs now sag in
Do you mourn them-- do you know
Who slew the U.S. Dragons?

Betty Jo Cartier

SAFETY'S SAKE--
FOR HEAVEN'S SAKE

One day St. Peter opened the gates
    In answer to a knock outside,
And asked the man who stood there dazed,
    What happened that you have died?

I've been a railroad man for thirty years
    And I thought I knew all the rules,
But it only took one fatal step
    To prove I was just like the other fools.

If I had the chance, I'd listen next time
    To try and learn all I can,
For safety's important to everyone
    And not just for the other man!

St. Peter just shook his head in despair
    As he beckoned the man to come in,
Some fellows never learn, he said to himself,
    They think they'll always win.

The door went shut, but it wasn't too long
    'Till the familiar knock came again,
For there's always a few who won't follow the rules
    And end as dying and broken men.

So I hope you men who are here today
    Will take the advice that I give,
For I know you want to enjoy a long life,
    So be careful -- for safety's sake -- and live!

Perry W. Snare

GHOSTS OF GLORY

Who are you roaring in the night,
Spewing hot flame with all your might?
Your roar has woke the town with sound.
Be still and let my sleep abound.

I hear Bessemer in dark of night,
Reflect on clouds my roar and light,
Providing jobs for you to work
All day long and through the night,
Your sweaty faces glow so bright.

Bessemer, I see you at dawn of day,
Coating me with summer snow gray.
Small flakes flutter, drift, and glitter.
Hold your spewing, no more litter!

I made good steel, you bought it too,
You stopped my draft one day, that's true,
When my vigor was at its prime.
Silenced my roar, quenched my flame,
It cost you jobs, now who's to blame.

Red clouds are monstrous at midday!
There is no sun in sky's array!
Your stacks do belch a dense smoke screen.
Hold your bad breath, let sun be seen.

I hear Open Hearth with lances blowing,
More and better steel heats making.
You did your part with work and sweat.
Setting records, produced the best.
For that you have a house to bless.

Your Coke Plant smell of afternoon,
from your bowels over town strewn.
I gasp for breath! Lungs burn with pain!
Clean your discharge! Clear acid rain!

My Coke Plant smell of afternoon?
You forced its cleaning, time not opportune!
Reduced the stink, doing it your way!
The cost too high, and market fell.
I chose retirement, and said farewell.

Smell fresh air; sky clear at sunset.
Where are you monsters, at sunset?
Crisp shadows fall long on empty land.
Bent figures form lines, where you did stand.

Monster at sunset, we do not hear!
You do not speak, you are not here!
But o'er empty fields, in building shells,
on misty nights and dreary days,
we see your Ghosts of Glory arrays.

Keith Barkett

JEANNETTE BLAST FURNACE
Detail

178

Jim Villani

MOMENT IN BRONZE

Written for the dedication of George Segal's sculpture,
The Steelworkers, in downtown Youngstown, April 1980

The Silent Forms

These are silent forms, the steel masters,
Their footsteps muffled, their roar deafened.
Discarded myths, theater of silhouettes
With keen eyes of metal,
The distance between their shadows
Cluttered with tools, lunch boxes,
Time Clocks washed orange, mock coveralls,
And down along the timid river
The orange bears, the friends of poems,
Rummage through the abandoned
Litter of Industrial America.

All is dark now. The chemistry of commerce
Is a dim memory. The bears go their lonely
Way along the river, the sunset burning
On the western river, and their fingers
Roll over the red dust of the silent forms,
The furnace that our fathers built.

Heavy Metal at Gun Point

The times are calciform--
A testimony to freeways and barrooms,
To the hot tension of billboards,
To nocturnal hamburgers, to dry heaves,
To the bright glare of street lamps
And public hallucinations,
To abandoned shopping carts and fragments
Of buildings, to solid waste and
Flat beer, to the rendezvous
With the soft tease of your eyelashes,
Your habitual cough,
Your slingshot delivery,
Your vanity magazines,
Your sweet tooth and sour disposition,
Your tarnished metal underpinnings,
And the burning gases on the horizon,
The red sky of my memory, the black rain,
The peculiar shapes rolling out of the tireless
Furnace, how she worked day and night without
Stopping, the air charged with bristling
Red sparks; I still see them, feel them,
Those giant cups of molten iron,
The shears, the great clippers,
The roasting of pigs, the flues,
The bucket like ladles, the striping molds,
The cranes, the soaking pit,
The blooming mill rolls, the monster wringer
Squeezing and flattening the hot ingots,
Thinner and thinner, at the salty command
Of the Roller in his orange pulpit,
Egging his metal thirst to the roughing mills,
To the last scissors, and the circular saws.

Their Moment in Bronze

The last days of the city ring with applause.
The taste of metal is gone from my mouth.
The people drink blue sky,
Bathe in the yellow wax sun,
Run with the silken wind.
This is the city of tenacious dreams,
The city of artisans, the city of common cause,
The city of new beginnings,
The city of saints, the city of workers,
How I remember them,
How I pity their reluctant agony
And their impromptu dismissal,
How I train my ambitions to follow in their footsteps,
How I revel in their achievements,
Their iconic austerity, their energized space,
Their homespun philosophies,
Their reasonableness of life,
Their sentimental traditions, their humanism,
Their moment in bronze.

The steel masters have rolled away.
Their coarse skin, their beards, their
Target eyes, their hot chill, their
Bitter homilies are stiffened
In the cast of time past.
Praise be their memory.
Praise be their *Moment in Bronze.*

Keith Barkett

JEANNETTE BLAST FURNACE

J. Richard Rowlands

JEANNETTE BLAST FURNACE

The Mahoning Valley and Youngstown for 150 years was one of the country's most important steel making centers. The remains of this industry are all but gone today; the last of the region's historic mills, even as I compose these paragraphs, is in process of being dismantled: the Jeannette Blast Furnace at the Youngstown Sheet and Tube Brier Hill Works. A monument to our industrial heritage, we capitulate to bureaucrats and property planners, allow another piece of living history to be erased. Even a popular recording artist, Bruce Springsteen, chimes his concern and reverence, "My sweet *Jenny*, I'm sinkin' down, here darlin' in Youngstown."

Built in 1918, Jeannette, named for the daughter of the president of Brier Hill Steel Company, operated for five years for this concern and fifty-four years for Youngstown Sheet and Tube, ultimately making over eleven million tons of iron for the production of *Youngstown* steel. This amount would be enough to build 275 Iowa class battleships or over 42,000 miles of mainline railroad trackage.

A blast furnace is a vessel that smelts iron ore into molten iron, called hot metal, which is then converted into steel. Iron ore, coke, and limestone are fed into the top of the furnace, and a 1,000 degree F blast of hot air produced by four hot blast stoves is fed into bottom. JennY could produce from 800 to 1,000 tons iron per day, and was one of twenty-one such furnaces that once lined the Valley from Warren to Lowellville.

The unique visual aspects of the tall furnace, skip hoist, and hot blast stoves are readily associated with the steel industry, and blast furnaces have become the universal symbol of iron and steel. In the Mahoning Valley tens of thousands of laborers worked at these furnaces and rolling mills producing the steel to build a community and a nation.

Blast furnaces were generally given names, since once put into operation they took on a life of their own, operating continuously for a "campaign" that could last several years. Just like humans, blast furnaces required food, water, and air to survive. They excreted wastes, and each had its own distinct personality or operating characteristics. Blast furnaces can become sick, too. A blast furnace superintendent's job rivals the doctor trying to make his patients well.

Jeannette made her last iron in September, 1977. From then till now she has become a symbol of a lost way of life. But she is much more than that. Today, Jeannette's passing eliminates the oldest modern blast furnace in existence, an item that might have had the potential to stimulate economic development in the Mahoning Valley once again, in the vision and mission of the short-lived Jeanette Blast Furnace Preservation Association. The Furnace Preservation Association lost their (our) battle to save and preserve a relic. The group does not give up, though, in its quest to retain homage to the Valley's industrial heritage. Yes, "Jenny" is gone, but technological relics are littered and abandoned throughout the region. The "Tod Engine," a device of profound consequence, has been acquired by the Association, after being located inside what was once Youngstown Sheet & Tube's blooming mill building in the Brier Hill works. The 1913 William Tod cross compound rolling mill steam engine worked for sixty-five years making rounds for the manufacture of Youngstown seamless pipe. The 34 inch x 68 inch x 60 inch engine was capable of producing up to 7,000 horsepower with its two large pistons and 20 foot diameter flywheel. The seamless rounds issued by the engine were fashioned into Youngstown's number one product, orange band seamless pipe. The Tod Engine is fully a monster, too, weighing in at over 200 tons.

What is now proposed to become the Youngstown Iron and Steel Museum will preserve this technological monument, additional iron crafting artifacts, and even railroad artifacts. The Association, which has made application to become a chapter of the national Society of Industrial Archaeology, sees a museum exhibiting the Tod Engine, a blooming mill exhibit, a merchant mill exhibit, a steel industry railroad exhibit, a freight rail exhibit, and a passenger rail exhibit. The Mahoning Valley was an industrial giant; homage to heritage is deserved and appropriate. Young's Town became Steel City in the popular imagination. This a place where rocks were turned into steel with fire, a place where every person in the Valley can trace one's roots.

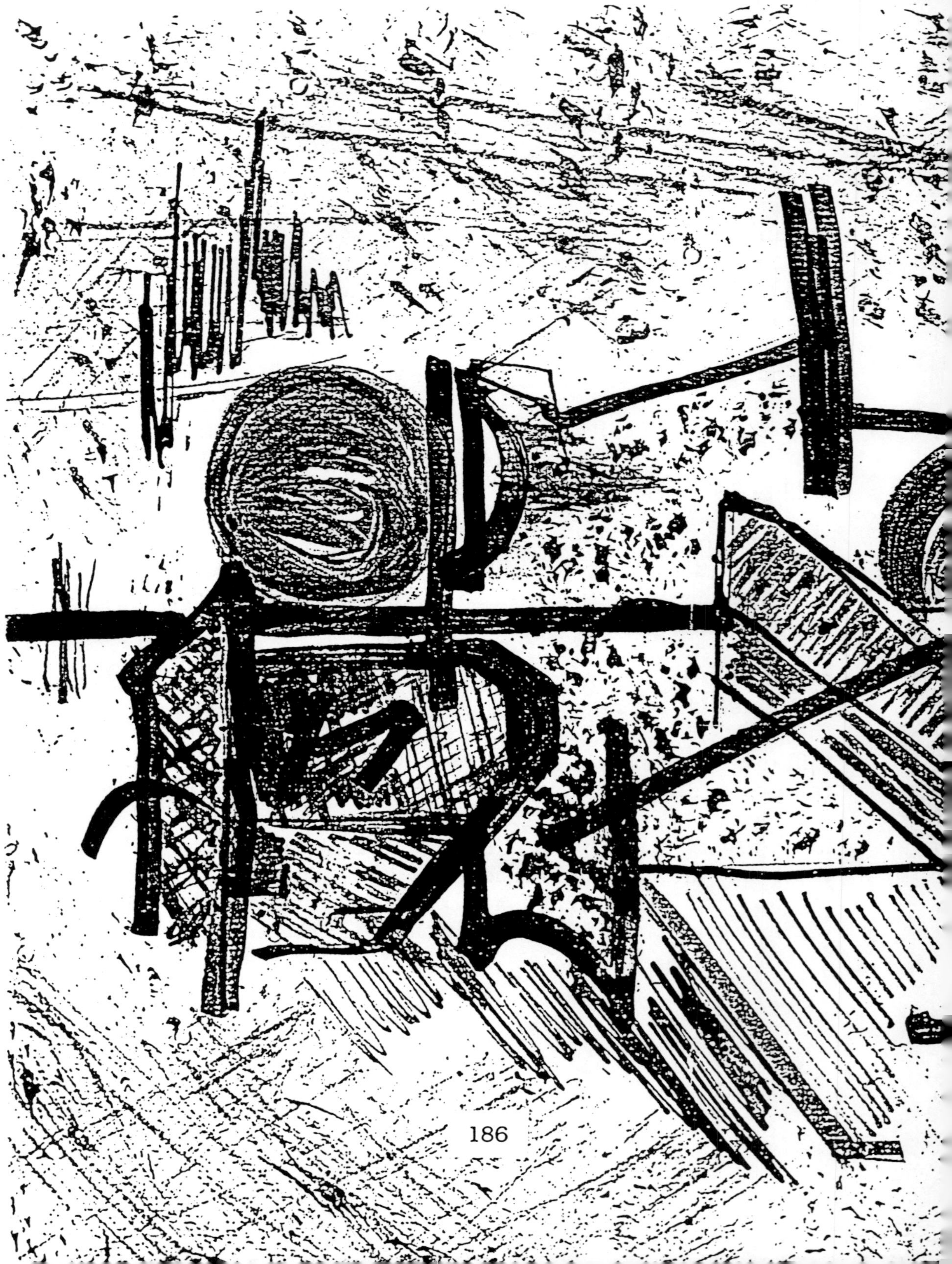

187 Isabel Kiriazis

STEELWORKER'S DILEMMA

Pamela Sioux Featherston

VALLEY OF STEEL

Valley of Shadows -- Valley of Tears
Skeletons of old steel mills, old Jenny
Stands like blackened teeth against gray Ohio sky.
Once **Mahoning** meant beautiful, and our river flowed
With life, native Americans gathered black walnuts,
Buckeyes, and pine nuts, and they fished the *Beautiful River*, counseled at the Rock, and then the Industrial
Age visited our Valley, sluiced the coal of Nature's
Bounty, turned water mud brown, dead, oily, soapy--
An empty river.   But as our River died the Valley
Hummed and life was good! People worked, ate,
Breathed in the pink air of prosperity.
                                        Now--
The empty sentinels stand in silence, while the ghosts
Of the men who once worked the hell-fire of molten
Steel sing sadly in the quiet breeze of evening.
Laborers, long lost, mere memories in our **Valley of Shadows**, once proud men, now with weak, leaking,
Confused eyes and roughened hands, that hauled the
Steel, now reach out with shame, with anger to clutch
The hated food stamps to feed bewildered children.

Who knew it would end? Not the men in the food
Stamp line, not the women behind, not the children
Who played in the scattered debris of abandoned
Dreams, while empty mills look on, and windows, like
Bleak, black eyes, stare at the *Valley of Tears.*

Stephanie Hong Owen

OHIO SONG

In lazy Ohio to leave means never to return
or so you've been told.
And if the falling buckeyes
and plump sparrows follow you outside
this pummeled land, onto the doorstep
of another world, tuck the vision
away in some side-pocket.
Take the best parts without sorrow.

I know the faithfulness is hard,
like the way it is difficult to keep
a promise made to a child, but slowly you realize
turning away is the only attempt
worth making these days.

So the train's steel engine starts and ends
here in Ohio, and by daybreak
the tin sound soundless in your heart
will break as the train reaches.
the edge of the landscape.
And the final suicidal whistle
will follow you into dreams
across the Indiana border,
haunt you like Autumn
halfway into Chicago.

But realize this: the pain never goes away,
and to deny the Ohio dirt on your hand
is to say there is no God,
nothing worth dying for.

Mary Patricia MaGuire Foley

THE PUDDLER POET
YOUNGSTOWN'S LABOR LYRICIST

In 1880, a young Irishman named Michael McGovern brought his family to Youngstown. He was told there was work for puddlers at McCurdy's *Siberia Mill.* Michael wasn't your usual iron worker. For years, he had spent his free time composing verses-- poems about Irish legends, about love, and about laboring as a puddler.

Nearly a century before Bruce Springsteen immortalized the Mahoning Valley labor force with his musical tribute *Youngstown,* Michael McGovern was a lyricist who championed the laborer in his poems and essays. Known throughout the country as the *Puddler Poet,* he used his Irish gift with words to create verses which depicted the toil and tribulations experienced by those men who made their living in the mills. With the soul of a poet, the dedication of a proud tradesman, and the anger of any Irishman against injustice, Michael wrote words that touched the hearts of workingmen and twinged the consciences of the industrial capitalists. The Irish immigrant became the Mahoning Valley's beloved poet.

His journey from Ireland to the United States was

similar to the experiences of many others who sought a better life for their families. Michael was born in Castlerea, County Roscommon, Ireland in 1848. The Ireland of his youth was a bleak land, crushed by political oppression and economic depression. He experienced firsthand the impact of *The Great Hunger*, Ireland's infamous famine. As a youth, Michael was apprenticed to a shoemaker. These were not the best of times for a tradesman. When people could barely afford food, they certainly could not afford to have shoes repaired. Michael went to England in the late 1860's, hoping to improve his trade skills and his income. In 1872, he married Annie Murphy. Life was not easy for these transplanted Irish, since the British still regarded them as "trouble." In 1875, with the sponsorship of a relative, Michael and Annie brought their young family to Allentown, Pennsylvania. Michael went to work in the rolling mills as a puddler. A few years later, the McGoverns came to the Mahoning Valley.

Michael was a puddler for over thirty-three years. A puddler working at the **Old Siberia** mill would routinely work twelve to fourteen hour shifts. When the shifts changed at the end of the week, he could work a continuous twenty-four hours. The puddler was a skilled tradesman who worked in front of the mill furnace, pulling the molten iron from the inferno with his tools and working it in 200-pound balls on the furnace hearth. This required enormous physical endurance, an understanding of the processes involved in molding iron, and a knack for timing the different steps of the puddling process. In those days, the puddler was not paid a standard hourly wage. He was paid a price for what he produced, and that price varied from mill to mill. The workers were at the mercy of the mill owner. As working conditions and wages became more inconsistent, the workers banded together to deal with the mill owners. Labor unions were their only hope for equity and fair treatment.

As the iron and steel industry grew in the U.S., the labor unions also increased and expanded. Workers showed their union pride in various ways. Michael McGovern expressed his through poetry. Michael had very little formal schooling, but he loved reading and literature. He had a natural gift for lyrics and rhyme, and expressed his ideas, his frustrations, and his pride in verses. He was proud to be a puddler, and he immortalized iron workers and their struggles. He frequently submitted poems to the two Youngstown papers, *The Vindicator* and *The Telegram*, to *The Gaelic American*, and to *The Amalgamated Journal*, a union publication. In 1899, he published *Labor Lyrics and Other Poems*, a collection of his works.

In the introduction to *Labor Lyrics*, Michael explains the uniqueness of the poems and the poet, "the product of a puddler of thirty-three years' standing in rolling mills, and whose life's school-term might be numbered by some few months. Puddlers are a boastful class of workmen. I, therefore, in keeping with their dignified practice make the boast that I consider myself the only puddler that ever stood on '*Top of earth*' who had the daring to issue a volume of poems." Michael's poems present many facets of the working man. In the first poem in the volume, "The Rolling Mill," his words paint a picture of the booming rolling mill as the pumping heart of the Mahoning Valley. He describes the thundering sounds, the fiery furnace, the smoking stacks. And he describes the mill from the perspective of those who depend on it for their livelihood:

> There's confidence where ev'ry stack
>   Sends forth its fiery blaze;
> Each mill-note which the hills throw back
>   Financial fear allays.
> Like songs that chords of gladness strike
>   Where troubles would but kill;
> There's nothing cheers the people like
>   The coughing of the mill.

Yet, most of his verses protest the plight of the working man at the mercy of the bosses, the "rulers of the mills." He constantly warns laborers of the value of their union in dealing with the industrialists. In "Squeezing His Lemons," Michael recounts a long tale of a mill owner who tries to force his workers to sign individual wage agreements instead of voting on a contract as a union:

> He stood before his working men
>   As ruler of the mills;
> Who lived among the "upper ten"
>   And sneered at labor's ills,
> And bid them come to meet him in
>   His office one by one,
> To sign a new "agreement; then"
>   He said, "the mills will run."
>
> He added, "You are foolish if
>   In face of dire distress,
> You will refuse in manner stiff
>   To '*sign*' and work for less;
> For competition says you men
>   Must work for less per ton,
> So '*sign*' to roll my profits in,
>   And then the mills will run."

"I tell you he's an anarchist
   Who'd slash at freedom's throat,
Who'd call a meeting and insist
   This matter put to vote;
For I shall deal with each alone
   As with a Slav or Hun,
For 'neath no scale except my own
   Shall these industries run.'"

"So sign at once my ironclad,
   And by its laws be bound.
For scabs in numbers can be had,
   Who now are tramping round;
Renounce your foolish sentiment,
   And labor unions shun,
Then strikes shall never more prevent
   These mills a steady run."

For three chapters, the poem spins a tale of the workers who stay unified and of the terrible fate of the "scabs" who work for the industrialist after he locks out the union. At the end of the poem, the *ruler of the mills* lowers wages again until the workers are almost destitute while he enjoys "the wealth his human lemons had been squeezed of day and night."

   In earlier days in the iron and steel industry, the "*bosses*" weren't always considered the enemy. Many had worked the furnaces themselves. As the industry grew, younger men who concentrated on profit and loss became the supervisors. In his poem "A Dialogue on the Bosses," Michael compares the two styles of leadership and how the working men perceived them:

We're scorned since the bosses came
   With glasses, rings, and collars,
Who hold their men and mules the same,

For what they're worth in dollars;
And when they cut each other's price
    Will make us stand their losses,
By cutting wages down a slice,
    These college bred young bosses.

Give me the good old bosses who
    Would smoke and chew and holler;
Who'd break a pig or dig a flue,
    And help to chip a *collar*.
Who'd aid a fellow when not well
    And who'd roll up their sleeves, or
Pull off their shirts and give a spell
    At furnace, rolls, or squeezer.

"Labor's Cause" was read at a labor mass meeting in Youngstown to show support for the Homestead strikers who were standing up to Andrew Carnegie at his Pittsburgh mill:

We meet today to sympathize
    With Homestead men who seek redress
To soothe with hope the widow's cries,
    And aim them in their sore distress;
To join in saying that as sure
    As reigns a supreme judge on high,
Who sees what men who toil endure,
    The cause of labor shall not die.

It was not Washington's intent,
    Whose patriot soldiers overthrew
Oppression that these states were meant
    As Eldorados for the few
Their fight is ours again today,
    Their wrongs and ours the same imply,
And in those patriots' names we say
    The cause of labor shall not die.

> Send forth the words on spirit wings
>   That wealth no longer shall maintain
> In this free land its petty kings,
>   With armed thugs to guard their reign.
> With justice in this noble fight
>   Wealth's private armies we defy;
> With votes as weapons wielded right,
>   The cause of labor shall not die.

When the workers of the Mahoning Valley were called to serve in the Spanish-American War, Michael paid tribute to them in "The Men of Riverside, O." The poem's second verse is an excellent example of his admiration for these laborers who became soldiers:

> We've thrown away the tools which we
>   Have used while making tin,
> And grasped the tools of war, and will
>   Some thousand battles win.
> For every seaman blown to death
>   Beneath Havana's tide,
> Some million Don's will fall before
>   The men of Riverside.

After the publication of his book, Michael continued to publish poems and essays in *The Vindicator* and the union papers. For a time, he published a daily verse in *The Vindicator*. When Michael McGovern died in 1933, the entire Valley mourned his passing. Stories on his death and the contributions he made during his life appeared on the front pages of *The Vindicator* and *The Telegram*. In an editorial, *The Vindicator* mourned the passing of its "oldest contributor." Similar stories appeared in *The Amalgamated Journal* and *The Gaelic American*. Friends and admirers, many from labor unions, formed a committee to raise funds for a monument to the beloved poet. Contributions were received from all over the country. The monument was placed at his grave in Calvary Cemetery in 1937. The stone, chiseled from Vermont granite, is a detailed replica of a puddling furnace with a large cross across the top. It still stands today.

Michael McGovern was my great-grandfather. When I was a young girl, my father would show me the grave and the monument when we visited the cemetery. My dad would tell me about the *Puddler* and the poems he wrote about the mills and the men who worked them. Since my father worked at Republic Steel, I knew his grandfather's writings were a source of pride for him. I was awed that one of my ancestors had made such an impact on his community and his contemporaries. My dad would point out the engraved tribute on the stone which proclaimed "A tribute from friends in seven states." And he would read the epitaph Michael wrote for his grave. It is etched in the bottom of the monument:

> Just place a rock right over me
>   And chisel there, that all may know it:
> Here lie the bones of M. McG.--
>   Whom people called "The Puddler Poet."

Works Cited

Michael McGovern. *Labor Lyrics and Other Poems.* Youngstown, Ohio: The Vindicator Press, 1899.

William Greenway

BETWEEN PITTSBURGH & CLEVELAND

What you notice first when you move
here is houses boarded like bandaged heads,
the ice-bound ships of empty steel mills,
old people sliding,
rusted cars spinning
through slush
that packs and blackens behind wheels,
drops, and lies in the road
like dead stars.

Next Sunday the Steelers play the Browns
but no one will watch--
we don't give one hundred and ten percent,
we don't take one game at a time.
We put on our pants one leg at a time,
and we sit on the bed to do it.
We're not going to rally
or regain the momentum.

Our sport is getting through the day,
the way in Scotland they run in only
jogging shoes up "fells," then back down
on paths of stones like bowling balls.

They say, we know this hill
can break bones.
We want to see if it will.

William Greenway

YOUNGSTOWN

We're new from the South to find
winter, the empty steel mills, even
in full sun, silhouettes, shadows

on the snow, of pyramids, Mayan
ruins, broken towers. Brown grass
brims in rusted buckets

like a drink. Tracks of coal
trains, ladders thrown
down. Southern winters

bleed in the rain. Here,
sheets cover the nude
corpse. Just to the

north Crane and Patchen
were born, to the south,
Wright, all dead too soon.

In spring we want to see
the glaze of land crack
like an egg, clouds

sluice from the sky like
silt from a creek, ruts of snow--
cold water, silver

            rails, take invisible
            things away, across ocher
            fields, into dark woods.

Bill Koch

LUNCHTIME SPECIAL

they discuss the days of Youngstown's manhood
when guys really named Blackie and Dutch
exerted the force of their character
against the weight of boiling metal
A muscular mill legend
could actually lift huge steel coil
and balance it over his shoulder
they grimace and pantomime the effort
most men needed to move it an inch
then they accept more coffee
conversation tracing a route
established as the ellipses of coins
riding the fiberglass wishing well
The waitress maintains a nurturing smile
and they try not to appear desperately grateful
for the warmth of the cup

Frank Polite

TAKE THE YOUNG OUT OF YOUNGSTOWN

  Since the name of Youngstown will soon be linked with "penitentiary" -- a Supermax no less -- I seriously propose that we consider changing our city's name.
  Historically, cities great and small, under the gun of some pressure or necessity (political, economic, spiritual), have changed their names. New York City was once New Amsterdam, Bombay is now Mumbal, and Istanbul, as we know, was Constantinople. There's nothing new or radical in this. It goes on all the time.
  It's time for "Young's town" to get out from under the gun, to change into, say, Mill Creek Park, Ohio, or Volney Rogers, Ohio. A change of name signifies a new beginning, afresh understanding, a determination

to enter into a new order.

Why continue to perpetuate Mr. Young's name? What has been his contribution, aside from the fact that he hiked over here from Whitestown, New York a couple of hundred years ago, sold off his parcel of land (double-dealing some of it) for a considerable profit, and then split from this area, never to return?

Whereas Volney Rogers gave us a true legacy, our once and future treasure, Mill Creek Park. The memory of Mr. Rogers has been respected and honored here for a long time. His statue is in the center of our city, off Glenwood Avenue, and a beautiful statue it is, pleasing to all who see it.

Where is a statue of John Young? If there is one, I've never seen it. If there isn't one, well, who cares? And chances are, those who might care, who retain nostalgic sentiments for Mr. Young's name, have long since, like him, run away into the suburbs.

We all know that changing a name or a label doesn't change what's inside, and that's fine. What's inside of our city is a caring and very charismatic people. A direct, honest people, utterly lacking in pretension. We are famous for returning home because, frankly, we can't stand to stay away from each other too long. Our ethnic mix has created a city of profound family values, a famous work ethic, and, as a New York magazine once noted, "the most beautiful women in America," not to mention its construction, banking, and legal savvy, its poets and artists, and its athletes.

But "Young's town"?

Let's face it; it is a terrible burden we no longer need to carry. It is a name that is indelibly associated with dead steel mills, with "Murdertown, U.S.A.," with tough town, with rust belt, and soon, with Youngstown

Penitentiary. Recently, *The Vindicator* quoted a state corrections official as saying that, "If prisoners in our system misbehave, we will warn them that they will be sent to Youngstown."

Warned about being sent to Youngstown? Do we need this? I agree that we need the prison. The bottom line is that we need jobs. What we don't need anymore, and good riddance, I say, is "Young's town."

Let us rename ourselves, or not. Put the question to the school children. Let them write essays. Put it on the ballot. Let us vote. My guess is, there's no popular support or sentiment for "Young's town," but a real desire for a name that restores us to our true heritage, the open beauty of our land and the open kindness of our people.

We could be Lake Cohasset, Ohio, or Lake Glacier, Ohio, or Volney Rogers, Ohio, or Mill Creek Park, Ohio, or Pig Iron, Ohio. Myself, I like Volney Rogers, Ohio, but that decision wouldn't be up to me.

Our institutions, so named, can retain the name of Youngstown if they choose. Or not. Youngstown State University might substantially raise its enrollment as, say, Volney Rogers State University. Our newspaper can continue to wave its distinguished banners as *The Vindicator*. The Youngstown Club can move its location to Poland or Canfield or Boardman where most of its members live anyway.

There just won't be a Youngstown anymore.

Glenn Sheldon

REASONS FOR MAPS

Pausing under the trestle
in downtown Youngstown,
I wonder where passenger
trains stop these days, for
last month the last one
here stopped. Always
there are fewer reasons
for maps; let dead town
stand still and no train
whistles disturb that peace.

*May no sweaty strangers
arrive accidentally!*

For my birthday last
week and for the empty
walls of my temporary
apartment in Toledo,
a friend gave me one
of those maps of the bottoms
of seas, the peaks and valleys
under all the earth's water.

Now if I walk north and
away from Ohio,
*I have the name
of somewhere
specific to go.*

George Peffer

LAUNDROMAT/FOUND POETRY

The third time this month
The woman
With the hair like the tree of life
And I are here. She is the queen
Of the *Laundromat* and winks:
    "Maybe our clothes are trying
to tell us something . . . "
I peer into the jumble of my laundry
Looking for a message.

An old man in a black baseball cap
Is folding sheets.
At the back of his cap
A tag is visible.
His hat size?
I move closer. No. It says $2.97
I tap the shoulder
Of the queen of the laundromat--
Pointing to the old man
I say, "He has a price on his head."

Roger Jones

SPECIAL PEOPLE

When I'm miles away from Youngstown,
On vacation,
Wallowing in where I am and what I am,
I'm a bit less than what I really am
    day in day out,
        because I'm on vacation in the old U.S. of A.
    no serious deviations,
        don't shave, a softer walk, look under rocks,
        grin a lot, bantering with any and all,
And people ask, "Where are you from?"
And I say, "I'm from Youngstown, Ohio,"
And they say, "Oh!"
Just like that, they say, "Oh!"
I have a decision to make,
An important people decision to make.

People are more important than most things,
So how should I speak to an "Oh!" response,
To a statement as fine as "I'm from Youngstown, Ohio,"
Travelling hither and yon.

And how could I not be so pleased,
Enjoying the view, enjoying the new,
Knowing that when I return,
I will be with Youngstowners,
People who sparkle, who know who they are,
People who know when you're full of it
And are happy to tell you.

So how do I react to the "Oh" sayers?
Some,
I toss off, let them be on their way,
What little that's there shouldn't be disturbed;
Some,
The sensitive ones,
Linger.
We smile and banter, talk of home and family,
Touch each other's hearts, glide pleasantly on.
When we part with a warm wave
And I say again, "I'm from Youngstown, Ohio,"
They say, "How nice to have known you,"
And they say, "People from Youngstown must be quite special,"
And I say, "Yes, quite special."

E. G. Hallaman

NO OBOE

There will be no oboe for the poets
at the First Unitarian Church--
the information was left with my son
who wrote dutifully on the scratch
pad by the phone.
I saw it there that night
when I got home. My heart, heavy
with a hundred small defeats, broke.
At dress rehearsal they said
I could have an oboe that would play
while I read my poems. I, the son
of an illiterate steelworker,
plagued by insecurities, unknown, un-
sung, discovered in the twilight
of my years, would have music to go
with my songs. How impressive,
I thought, an oboe wailing just off
stage while I read there on Elm St.
a hundred Unitarians with shivers up
their spines. But half way through
the week, on a day the world
closed in to demand surrender, I
came home and with my coat still on
I saw the message by the phone:
"There will be no oboe for the poets
at the First Unitarian Church."

Suzanne Kane
Butler Museum

Diane Drapcho

DANCING WITH DR. ZONA

As I scan the glitzy invitation
for the big shindig at the **Butler**
(opening night -- Tony Bennett's exhibition), it starts.
By the time I reach the
date and dinner entrées,
it's way beyond my control--
I'm steppin' out . . . .
Steppin' out with my baby,
can't do wrong 'cause I'm in right.
It's for sure, not for maybe
that I'm dressed up tonight . . . .
I can see Dr. Zona in the center of the atrium
looking dashing and debonair,
all decked out in his Matisse-inspired
matching cummerbund and tie.
Like a young Fred Astaire, lithe and charming,
mingling and maneuvering to a mambo rhythm,
he effortlessly moves across the marbled floor
--his eyes ever searching--
he makes his way through the crowd to
the gleaming staircase where
he reaches for the gloved hand I gracefully
hold outstretched. Serene and statuesque
(like the sublime Audrey Hepburn expecting Rex)
I stand, waiting for his escort.
Acknowledging his arrival with a doelike glance,

I descend the remaining steps
and immediately we start to sway
(in a syncopated time)
to Tony crooning *You Go To My Head.*
"I love this song," I gush;
he whispers, "I know."
You go to my head
and you linger like a haunting refrain
and I find you spinning 'round in my brain
like the bubbles in a glass of champagne . . . .

My mind reels as I realize:
I'm dancing with Dr. Zona!
He smells wonderful I notice
as his arm clinches around my waist,
pulling me in closer in preparation
for a spin. As we twirl about Beecher Court,
the artwork takes on a kaleidoscopic effect
that makes me feel even more intoxicated.
"Tony's work has never looked better," I whisper.
We're gliding from gallery to gallery,
we're cheek to cheek; heaven, I'm in heaven,
and my heart beats so that I can hardly speak--
and I seem to find the happiness I seek
dancing cheek to cheek . . . .
we dip!

The drink I dribble down my blouse
brings me back to reality
and I toss the invitation in the trash.

Tony won't even sing, anyway!

Nancy Bizzarri

THE CITY OF NO RETURN

So the residents of
the City of No Return
read in Sunday installments
The Trouble With Youngstown,
they follow the exploits
of their brave mayor as
he battles to save poor
attorneys from the evil
clutches of the "Hotdog Lady,"
they gasp as he calls her,
"full of baloney,"
they wince as he
tells university experts
that he has nothing
against plans, that,
in fact, he has thirty.

They read that
the University
is hosting an
Other Ohio
conference.
They learn that
Youngstown is on the other side
of the Other Ohio.

They fold their
papers in their
laps and dream
of the Other Ohio . . .

Where doctors'
daughters have
nice haircuts
and flawless skin,
where grandpas sit
on white Victorian
porches and wax
eloquent about lemonade,
and everyone
has a new car
with bumpers
and four working
headlights.

Where is this
Other Ohio?
It must be beautiful.
It must be where
you go when you die
because they have known
people who have left here,
and you never hear
from them again,
not even a postcard,
and they never come back.

Soon there will be
no one left to ask
how to do things,
when to cut back
the roses and where
to pinch off the dead blooms.

Cynthia Booher

STARVATION
(in four parts)

I. *Avery reading* The Second Sex *while "socially working"*

    she moves quickly
    through their stories their excuses their lives there
    is no time no need to reflect   eats diet pills to keep
    from collapsing   she can be heard at office parties
    saying *I've slept with every man here*
                (no matter how many)
    chances are she has   she wears feminism like armor
    but can't make it work   she dreams of kissing
    the backs of deBeauvoir's knees as her sisters call
    out her name for the cause

II. *Lilith with plum sauce*

    she speaks Cantonese to impress says it
    inspires better tips   each night she drinks a little
    more to sleep not to dream   she has a child
    a daughter she will not speak of in her attic place
    in exile she entertains young men
          fledglings really
    drawn to her like a lodestone   her sentence is
    to chronicle every miserable thought
                      (there are so many)
    but when she writes the words come like
    zephyrs and the sacred nine stand outside
    the garden wall and call her name

III. Jane at fifty in white with guilt

    she answers *serious* to every question on
    the psychological evaluation   gross passivity ensures
    the fulfillment of her needs   (they are not many)
        interaction   distraction
    she knows little about the doting stranger who
    visits each day   only that the stranger brings
    cigarettes and that the stranger is good to her
    she regrets most but resolves nothing   she is too
    young to play proper widow   too old to play bride
    she wishes instead to disappear beneath the veil
            black or white
    and come out clean when she hears
    the groom call her name from the urn

IV. Tilda sore on a Sunday morning

    she sings Negro spirituals to her Sunday school class
    she lost two pints of blood the last time
    she was late   won't leave because of god
        and no money
    in church she cleans for Him   Murphy's Oil
    swirls sweet in swollen nostrils
    she owns ninety-nine Hummels and displays
    them proudly for visitors   (they are few)
    the hundredth will be an angel with stained
    glass wings   they come after the punishments
    so He never goes hungry   her eyes are squab
    grey though lifeless since '72 when He broke her
    ribs   her words whistle through uneven
    front teeth thanks to the banister
    that broke her last fall   she believes in right to
    life   even His
    as she waits patiently and listens for her
    name to be called

Terry Murcko

HEY BUDDY (A POLKA)

It's been three months in my new Liberty suburban home,
And my neighbor hasn't noticed I'm alive.
He was in his yard this morning as I left for work,
And he's still putzing there when I pull up the drive.

He's a lawn-care compulsive
Who worries about the weeds.
He'll push his power mower over dormant grass
Twice or thrice a week
To remind it what awaits
if ever it awakes.

At the corner of our house there is this big smoke tree
That my Linda loves to think of as her child.
When her mother tells her, "Trim it," she says, "Let it be
Wandering and willowy and wild."

But now this lawn-care compulsive
Who worries about the weeds
And confronts his fears with his pruning shears
Is pointing at its leaves.
They've crossed an invisible plane
And into this mower's domain.

"Hey Buddy, what're you gonna do about that tree...
"Or bush...or whatever you call it...
"What do you call it?"

"I call it the sky's vagina
"That you're not allowed to see;
"I call it the mask that its absence wears;
"I call it nearer my God than me;
"I call it one of many trees of knowledge you would like to prune,
"The roots of my name on the moon,
"The thousand fingertips of my attention on your secret joy,
"The forbidden tree of life in the womb;

"It's what's left of all the fog from the dawning of this world,
"A torch for the dying of a squirrel,
"The straw from which we, over here, sip the nectar of your fear,
"The smoke from the burning of a girl.
"Now some call it a revelation; and others, a miracle;
"Still others, an affirmation of something deeply meaningful;
"Or maybe it's a pain in the ass
"I guess I'll have to go inside and ask,
"Hey Buddy, what're we gonna do about that tree...
"Or bush...or whatever we call it...
"What do we call it?"

Now the lawn care compulsive
And the shell-shocked Mr. White
Sit in folding chairs in front of White's garage
Pondering the meaning of their fright.
We haven't done anything yet.
We're hoping that they don't forget
To ask about crabgrass...
We've got magnificent crabgrass...
We've got miraculous crabgrass...
We've got mythical crabgrass...
We've got cancerous crabgrass!

E. G. Hallaman

THEY CAME AT DAWN

They came at dawn
  from the southeast over 422--
  flying low soundless,
  a fleet of giant creamsticks.
They bombed the rusted mills
  in Campbell first,
  huge mushroom-shaped
  clouds of cream rose high
  toward the hills
  where people came out
  to watch the devastation.
They bombed Struthers,
  a ribs place
  that was to keynote
  Struthers' renaissance.
KBN weather was on,
  when it got hit "there's
  nothing significant on radar"
  were the last words heard.
The three drinkers at Irish Bob's
  didn't have a chance,
  they'd never hear *Merrimac,*
  Merrimac again.
Gutnecht Towers collapsed,
  the old people regretting
  they'd never get to vote against
  anything again.

As Federal Plaza filled with whipped
   cream, Sadie's croaking voice
   ordered CETA workers
   to clean it up.
YSU sustained direct hits,
   there were few student casualties,
   but a University spokesman said
   over 150,000 flowers and trees
   were withering.
The giant creamsticks
   floated toward Austintown.
   The bombing had stopped,
   leaving behind a valley
   filled with thick sweet cream.
The mayor left for Washington
   to get help.
   His aunt drove him to Pittsburgh
   to catch the plane.
The Ecumenical Coalition revived,
   promised to buy a mill
   and manufacture something
   out of the cream.
The Sierra Club analyzed the cream,
   decided it wouldn't
   hurt the rivers,
   but it shouldn't be smoked.
Ann Harris with fresh eye shadow
   bounded through the valley,
   stuffing whipped cream
   into mine shafts.

The Sokol Center baked cream puffs
   and the Health Department
   came to lunch.
The rackies took bets
   on the amount of cream that fell.
   Nobody won.

Time passed,
   the cream got cooked, eaten,
   packaged, and sold.
   The town glowed in prosperity,
   no one noticed,
   it was ephemeral -- it wouldn't last.
It's quiet now,
   the cream is gone.
   The mayor still goes to Pittsburgh
   to fly to D.C.
   The rackies still take bets
   and nobody wins.
St. E's is building a bridge toward
   Columbiana.
   Siegel is plotting another
   monument, and the Playhouse is doing
   a musical of *Grapes of Wrath*.

Will the giant cream sticks come again?
   Maybe they will.
   Youngstown waits and hopes.

Thomas P. Gilmartin, Sr.

LOSING YOU

Riverboat Gambling
Wants to come to our town
Who ever thought about that?
Our town is so pure
How could anyone think of it?

I play Bingo
On Monday Wednesday and Fridays
Go to the track on Saturdays
Play lotto Wednesdays and weekends
I'm broke-- going to church festivals
Taking chances on cars or split the pot

My credit card payments are overdue
Missed payments on the house
My luck has to change
Maybe the Riverboat
People will give me credit
What do I have to lose?

Susan Wojnar

THE GREEN MAN
A Mahoning Valley Folk Tale

  Certain aspects of the flavor and essence of the Mahoning Valley can only be expressed through those stories we grew up with and told ourselves and each other. Local folklore helped define our personal and cultural edges. Though there are many definitions of myth and folklore, such stories, with their told and re-told *outer-limits* qualities, often illustrate our borders and frontiers in order that we may move beyond them.
  Much of our local folklore involves recurring supernatural happenings or ghostly visages connected to the scene of some tragic death. The disturbing power and presence of the Mob in the Mahoning Valley is also chronicled in local folk tales. Many a forest-shrouded and desolate stretch of highway as well as several area swamps, often referred to in Mahoning Valley folklore as *Black Hand Country*, are the alleged site of mythic underworld murders, hangings, and body-dumpings.

Anyone who grew up in the Mahoning Valley undoubtedly spent some portion of their teenage years purposefully trying to scare themselves to death by seeking out face-to-face meetings with the bizarre or gruesome characters described in such folk tales. The pursuit of scary encounters became something of a local rite of passage.

For me, the most enduring and most fully developed folk tale from the "let's-grab-a-six-pack-and-drive-around-anticipating-an-encounter-with-the-supernatural-until-we-scare-ourselves-witless" category is the story of **The Green Man**. I've heard this folk tale for what seems like forever. The story never stayed static. It didn't change so much as it grew over time.

*

It was said he lived somewhere out in a run-down shack, out in the woods, at some indefinite locale between the Ohio and Pennsylvania border, about 20 miles east of here. He also had an indefinite age. All we knew for certain was that at some earlier time, it was indefinite when and how, he had a terrible accident that involved a high voltage of electricity which tragically disfigured his body and colored his skin with a luminescent, greenish hue. The Green Man was said to be horrible to behold.

Shunned by society due to his deformity, the Green Man became a recluse. Infrequent encounters with humanity supposedly resulted in The Green Man feeling shamed and forlorn by the anxiety and disgust he provoked in his distant neighbors. Time went by and his prolonged isolation gave rise to bitterness and anger towards those who were more fortunate than he in regards to physical appeal and skin tone.

It was said he stalked desolate stretches of forest-shrouded roads looking for victims to take his wrath and frustration out on. More often than not, motorists stranded in the middle of the night were the Green Man's favorite easy pickings. Though we all knew someone who knew someone who was personally attacked by The Green Man, it never prevented us from driving around on those desolate, forest-shrouded roads in the middle of the night. And that's all we knew about The Green Man when we went looking for him.

Eventually, we began to hear that someone knew of someone who had accidentally stumbled on The Green Man's place of residence. It was said The Green Man had made a grab for the unsuspecting intruder. Then it was said that The Green Man, in the horribly deformed voice we all knew he had, asked the intruder to please stay and visit with him awhile. It seemed all those alleged attacks on stranded motorists were highly exaggerated and misinterpreted. The Green Man was, after all, just a lonely guy. Attacking stranded motorists had become his only way of reaching out to touch someone.

After awhile, our perception of The Green Man changed. And all those someones who had shunned him and everyone who had been afraid of him began to feel really bad about their attitude towards him. We heard of people who were making pilgrimages to The Green Man's shack, bringing him gifts of supplies and food, or just making a point to stop by and pass the time of day with him. We all knew someone who knew someone who claimed to be a very close, personal friend of The Green Man.

There was a sense of awe that went along with knowing that someone had actually visited The Green

Man. It seemed such a remarkably chivalrous act. These unknown someones became Lords of Humanity for whom we had undying respect. We spoke of these known yet unknown people in hushed and reverent tones. "I heard that Danny visited The Green Man last weekend. Brought 'em a ham." Everyone cared about and had sympathy and compassion for the Green Man. We all wished that we, too, could be close personal friends of the Green Man or maybe just bring him a ham from time to time.

Green Man tales began to taper off, but every so often we would ask each other about the Green Man, in case someone might know someone who knew something new and interesting about him. "Heard anything about the Green Man? He still alive?" Nobody ever talked about being afraid of running into him on desolate, forest-shrouded roads anymore. In fact, we were all just a little disappointed that we hadn't come face to face with him ourselves. Other than the occasional ham-delivery tale, little was heard about the Green Man for what seemed like forever.

Then we heard the Green Man was gone. He had moved away. Too many someones were constantly over-running his shack. We heard that the tide of curiosity-seekers, pilgrims bent on undoing the wrongs done to him, had wearied The Green Man and he just moved on.

I haven't heard anything else about The Green Man for what seems like forever.

Michael Green
Keen Eye

Anita Gorman

MY FATHER'S RESTING PLACE

That my father should repose in Canfield soil
astonishes me; not only that I thought he'd never die,
but that of all the lands he'd been, this would outlast
them all: Sweden, Chicago, Canada, Minnesota,
New York, Ohio: my father never found the perfect place,
restless always, looking around the corner,
over the next hill, for Shangri-La.
Now he lies near the road to other towns,
by a little girl and an old man,
over the next hill from the youth who fell
in the Battle of Atlanta,
around the corner from the village pioneers.

Irene Santon

FUTURED

Youngstown, you are a city possessed by predators
pressing sounds into the night; gunfire;
Citizens in flight, fearful;
Youngstown: murdertown, bombtown,
waiting for the last blast.

A city not quite dust, not yet ashes.

Your people grieve, the memories
clear, vivid; no more
open hearth fires, no more smoke-filled
skies of Steeltown: *Sheet and Tube,
Republic Steel, U.S. Steel,* no more
big band sounds:
*Nu-Elms, Idora Park Ballroom,
Palace Theater,* no more
Christmas crowd shopping:
*McKelvey's, Strouss-Hirschburg,
Livingston's,* no more
lunching: *Mural Room, Brass Rail,
Purple Cow,* no more,
no more, no more......

And yet,
Youngstown, you are possessed by prophets
proclaiming a new dawning: visions,
Citizens standing firm, hopeful.
Youngstown: comebacktown,
waiting for the next big boom.

A city reborning, not yet renaissance.

The struggle is legend; survival is celebrated:
*The Rayen School, Butler Institute of Art,
Stambaugh golf course.*
The present real: *Lyden House, Powers Auditorium,
Federal Court House, B&O Station.*

Celebrate, ***Youngstown***, your 200th year,
Celebrate, ***Youngstown***,

                    what was

                              what is

                                          what will be.

Helen Shagrin

LIFE'S TAPESTRY

Life can be compared to a tapestry
Woven each day at a time.
The pattern fashioned by our doing
of things, either negative, helpful, needed or fine.

I hope that my tapestry be woven
With thoughtful, loving care
So that when I come to the finish
A worthy one, people shall declare.

And may I in the weaving
Find the challenges of daily life
Not too great to be taken in stride
And each day's efforts seem just right.

Then shall the work be joyous
Though some days brighter by far,
But the fact that I still can be weaving
Should make me most grateful to God.

May I show gratitude by continuing
To design a pattern that flowers.
And may that which still lies ahead
Be woven in peace and understanding in happy hours.

Isabel Kiriazis
Calendar Art

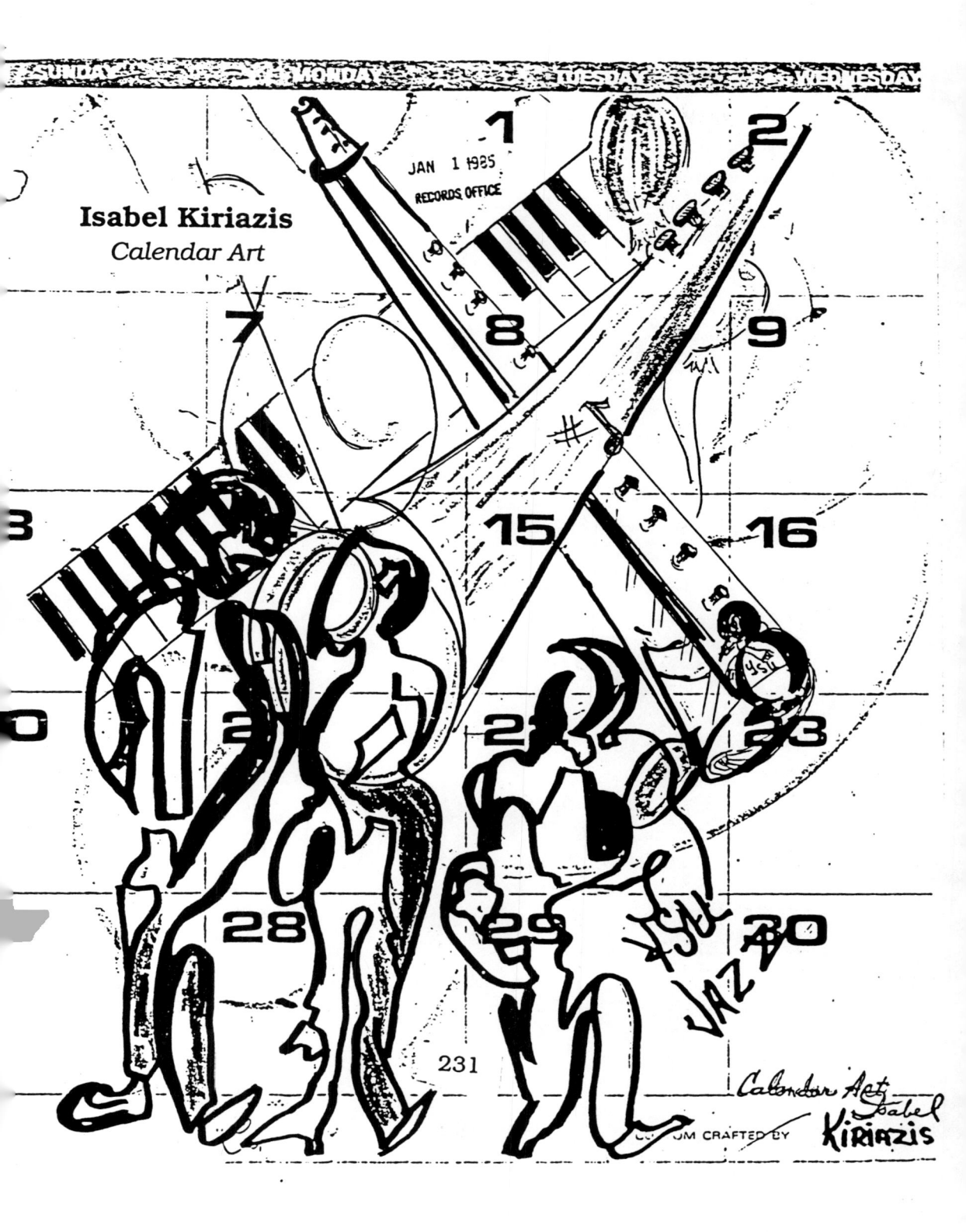

Mahoning Valley Writer Series

PIG IRON PRESS